"Food is something we all have in common. It is a basic need and a central part of our lives, communities, and cultures. Reflecting over her ongoing journey as a parent, professor, community farm manager, neighbor, and more, McMinn artfully weaves stories, Scripture, science, and recipes together in this holistic and practical exploration of what it can look like to eat well today. This book is a celebration of God's goodness in the world and his loving provision for us and for all he has made. It is a warm and compelling invitation to a more compassionate, nourishing, and faithful way of living."

—**Ben Lowe**, Evangelical Environmental Network

"In *To the Table*, Lisa Graham McMinn brings together a delightful collection of stories, recipes, and philosophy about gardening, cooking, and everything in between. This whimsical little book provides a feast in many forms. It is a must-read for every gardener, cook, and person concerned about where our food comes from and how we gather to eat it."

—**Christine Sine**, Mustard Seed Associates

"Lisa Graham McMinn's *To the Table* is itself a practical feast. From its researched critique of the modern food industry to the way it describes our everyday practices and relationship with food as a spiritual experience, *To the Table* helps us regain the knowledge and intimacy necessary to eat well, to eat right, and to eat in communion with creation and each other. Whether you have decided to join the food hope movement for a better future or you are simply looking for personal renewal in the way you and your family eat, Lisa's book is the best place to begin."

—**Randy Woodley**, cosustainer of Eloheh Farm and author of *Shalom and the Community of Creation: An Indigenous Vision*

To the Table

To the Table

A Spirituality of Food, Farming, and Community

Lisa Graham McMinn

BrazosPress

a division of Baker Publishing Group
Grand Rapids, Michigan

Published by Brazos Press
a division of Baker Publishing Group
P.O. Box 6287, Grand Rapids, MI 49516-6287
www.brazospress.com

Printed in the United States of America

Library of Congress Cataloging-in-Publication Data
McMinn, Lisa Graham, 1958–
    To the table : a spirituality of food, farming, and community / Lisa Graham McMinn.
        pages cm
    Includes bibliographical references.
    ISBN 978-1-58743-370-2 (pbk.)
    1. Food—Religious aspects—Christianity. 2. Dinners and dining—Religious aspects—
Christianity. I. Title.
    BR115.N87M38 2015
    641.3—dc23   2015029280

Brandon Buerkle created the illustrations in this book.

16   17   18   19   20   21   22   7   6   5   4   3   2   1

To God's web of life that feeds us all—

I bow my head in awe and gratitude

Contents

Acknowledgments

Tell me a story and I will care more. Maybe it's a personal weakness, but I find it to be true. If you give me someone that I can see, then I can imagine that someone as a family member or a friend or neighbor. Since I'm not unique on this point, I asked several people to let me poke into their lives so I could include their stories. Thank you Kim, Sarah, Brandon, Michael, and Brenda for your willingness to entrust me with your stories and thoughts about how you feed your families and bake bread and pastries for your community.

Three women read this manuscript chapter by chapter as I wrote it, affirming, challenging, and responding as people with their own food preparation histories and thoughts on how food, politics, and faith collide and collude. Thank you Pamela Augustine and Carol Sherwood for the time you dedicated to this task, for your openness to these ideas and honest responses. I would like to offer an extra thank-you to Ada LaNeal Miller. Your probing questions and reflective connections and comments made this book better and more true.

Sherry Macy offered to read the manuscript with an editor's eye and taught me things that I didn't know about comma use, hyphenation, and other matters that make books read well. Speaking of editing, this book wouldn't have happened if Bob Hosack, my longtime friend, didn't have breakfast with me one morning to listen to how my heart and soul were being engaged and stretched. I'm grateful for the risk he took in publishing a book about food and for his encouragement and support throughout the process. The editing of Lisa Cockrel, Jennifer Jantz Estes, and Brian

Bolger made it stronger, more precise, and perhaps a *little* less rhapsodic, as Lisa might say. The behind-the-scenes work of the design team, production team, and marketing team turned words I arranged on the page into the book you hold in your hand. Thanks to all of you at Brazos/Baker.

I can't express adequately how deeply I appreciate Brandon Buerkle partnering with me by providing the illustrations for this book. We talked about what I hoped each chapter would communicate, and he'd send me drawings as he finished them. After he texted me the seed picture (so much tiny detail!), I texted back, "You make me weep." He responded, "I'm sorry it was that bad. I'll start over." But he knew what I meant. I weep because his illustrations capture something deeply beautiful; he says in pencil and ink what I am trying to say with words.

Finally, every morning I wake up to a man who is many things to me, in addition to being my husband. Mark is the father of my children, grandfather of our grandchildren, and also my co-farmer, my sous chef, and the head pastry chef in our home. Mark is always my first reader and best critic. He is bold and fearless in his critique and generous with his affirmation, and I love him for that, among other things. Living with him these thirty-six years has shaped me profoundly.

Introduction

Coming Back to the Kitchen

Food is nothing less than Sacrament.

—Leslie Leyland Fields[1]

Every December of my childhood, three sugary treats showed up during the holidays: Sandies (also known as Russian Tea Cakes—an absolute favorite), Divinity (a supersweet candy popular in the 1960s and 1970s that I did not like *at all*), and Hello Dollies (which I liked rather too much). These cookies, candies, and bars were as much a part of our holiday tradition as Dad placing tinsel on the tree, strand by strand, politely insisting that our help was not needed. My recipe for Sandies is typed on an index card and stored, along with other relics, in a green plastic box I acquired in a high school home economics class. I preserved this particular recipe with a plastic sheath made for such purposes, but still it's blotched with bits of butter that seeped onto the card before I decided to preserve it.

• *Sandies* •

1 c.   softened butter

2 tsp.   water

⅓ c.   sugar

2 tsp.   vanilla

2 c.   sifted flour

1 c.   chopped hazelnuts (or pecans)

1 c.   powdered sugar

Cream butter and sugar. Add water and vanilla and mix well. Blend in the flour and nuts, cover, and chill for at least four hours. Preheat oven to 325 degrees.

Roll dough into 1-inch balls and bake on an ungreased baking sheet for about 20 minutes. Cookies should not brown, except perhaps on the bottom. Transfer to cooling racks and cool completely. Roll in powdered sugar to coat. Cookies will stay fresh for 2–3 days in an airtight container, and they freeze well.

At some point during high school (probably for that home economics class), I typed out recipes on cards. No doubt I was thinking of my hope chest, which is not only an antiquated idea these days but perhaps a bit offensive as well. On my Sandies recipe the typed word *filbert*, which is what we called hazelnuts back then, drifts up, letter by letter, toward the word *pecans* above it. While this may be a quirk of the manual typewriter, the word drifts with emphasis, an assertion that filbert ought to be the nut of choice, rather than pecan.

Auden and Juniper, both five years old, have helped me in the kitchen for several years already. They drag the black chair from the dining room so they can stand counter-high and pour, stir, and lick. When they started helping, mostly (if it was allowed) they licked.

A few years ago, while three-year-old Auden waited for me to come to her house to pick her up for our Sandies baking date, her mom overheard her talking to herself saying, "It is so *unexpected* that I get to bake with Grammy today!" As her mother tells the story, Auden was speaking with much enthusiasm, as though she'd not been to my house already on countless occasions to bake. Still, it made me smile. After rolling the balls and putting them in the oven, we sat down for our traditional mocha/hot chocolate break. She wanted to do "cheers" by smashing our mugs together, which we do often enough, but because I had pulled out the fancy tea set, I taught her how to do pinky cheers with our little fingers instead. We started calling each other "Madam," and I taught her to drink with one pinky in the air, which was dangerous in terms of spilling hot chocolate, which she did. At any rate, she told me I was a "cool girl." I haven't been called that in a long while.

To the Table is about getting people together in the kitchen and around tables—children and old folks, men and women, friends and family. It's about dusting off ideas about food that haven't been examined for a while and taking a good look at them. I invite readers to remember what they have loved about food and have thought about farmers; I urge them to rethink the word *drudgery*, as in "cooking is drudgery." Together, we will look at food from all sorts of angles, including those that take our gaze inward, outward, and upward.

If that sounds like too much attention on too insignificant a part of life, let me say up front that I thought the same at an earlier stage in my life. But I am reminded of the importance of food when I go hiking and pack too little food for too long a day. Or when, on rare occasion, I pass on breakfast and lunch and dinner. A spring day loses its brilliance; my husband, Mark, becomes annoying; and even coworkers and friends become less, well, wonderful. If I go too long without food, I stop thinking clearly, and I don't have the energy to fulfill obligations or to pursue what brings me joy. If I continued in this manner, I'd eventually stop being altogether.

Every human activity accomplished in a day gets accomplished because people consume food. Eggs and pancakes, grilled cheese, tomato soup and apples, fish, asparagus, and baby red potatoes keep bodies warm, hearts pumping, and brains sending messages this way and that.

For many years, the growing, harvesting, transporting, and processing of food remained on the periphery of my consciousness, comfortably just outside my awareness. I ate tomatoes and strawberries in January and bought the occasional hamburger and french fries at fast-food restaurants, unaware of the steps it took to get food from field to mouth. I started hearing about and reading that some ways of assuaging my appetite came at a more significant cost than I knew—not only to my body but also to my soul, our family's well-being, and the health of local and global communities.

Wendell Berry calls eating an agricultural act, by which he means that the choices we make reinforce the processes, for good or ill, that get food to our tables. In *Food and Faith*, theologian Norman Wirzba talks of eating as deeply spiritual and offers a thoughtful theology of food. Eating, he says, has the power to remind us daily of God's provisioning, a very earthy grace. Eating can call forth a reverence for God's creation and awareness of the processes that get food from seed to table. I no longer doubt that our relationship to food shapes how we understand ourselves, God, and our place in the world.

Over the last decade I started hungering for *good* food. This hopeful hunger is spiritual; choices I make about eating affect not only my soul but also my local and global neighbors.

So yes, food and faith are deeply intertwined. It ought not be surprising. After all, God appears throughout Scripture when people gather to eat. God causes food to grow, feeds the hungry, satisfies the thirsty, and establishes days for feasting—all reasons to celebrate God's goodness and faithfulness.

Mark and I said grace with our children mostly out of habit. Now they are grown and we still say grace. While habit is still involved, so is a growing awareness of some larger grace that is poured out on all creation. In our best moments we pause in gratitude before eating, recognizing food as God's sustaining grace and remembering our utter dependence on something outside of ourselves for our existence. Eating is a humble reminder that we are not, after all, autonomous beings; we are interdependent ones.

Grace offered at the end of the day as we sit at a table of food connects food to faith. What changes when we couple a spiritual discipline of gratitude with this basic rhythm of daily eating? Maybe we learn to better use moments connected to food to see God's bountiful love and grace and to respond in ways that move us inwardly, outwardly, and upwardly toward compassion and gratitude.

To the Table crafts space to allow God's spirit to move us toward celebration, gratitude, and compassion. By connecting values of love, hospitality, and justice to everyday choices at the grocery store and around our tables, we live out attentive gratitude. In the pages that follow I'll travel the path food takes, starting with food on the table and working backward to seeds in the hand.

I'm learning to eat well through conversations about food ethics and by embracing old food traditions. Most importantly, I'm stepping back into the kitchen and looking for good things to happen. When I invite others to join me there, we become creators of good food; we eat with intention and foster community at the table.

Michael Pollan suggests that growing, preparing, preserving, and eating food is one of the most worthwhile of human activities. Maybe communion with God happens as much through stocking our pantries with good and just food and by inviting others to our tables as it does in ascending the mountaintop or meeting God in the desert or at a retreat center.

After reading a draft of the introduction, my friend Ada wrote in the margin, "What Auden delightfully expressed in being *unexpected* probably carries out through the 'eating good' journey. Unexpected is exactly where I find myself in relationship to a good God. I am astonished at God's provision through food and eating; it's quite radical, and I don't know how to live it out on a daily basis."

To the Table is a journey both ordinary and full of the unexpected. This is a book of hope for a new generation responsible for feeding themselves and their families; it's also for those who have spent countless hours, satisfying or not, in kitchens. It is a book of hope for things longed for—for the very real spiritual and physical well-being that comes from living intentionally as we engage the daily tasks, challenges, and joys of eating.

Reflections and Questions

1. What was a favorite childhood food, and what memories do you associate with it? Taking this a step further, what would you need to make that food this week? Perhaps you need to track down the recipe, buy some ingredients, borrow a kitchen tool, or call a parent, sibling, aunt, uncle, or grandparent. If you share this food with friends or family, consider recounting to them an "I remember this . . ." story from your childhood.

2. What kinds of feelings do you have toward food-making? Below is a list of possibilities. Reflect and perhaps journal or talk in a group about when and why you feel as you do. What makes your feelings change from one day or situation to the next? How have your overall feelings about cooking changed in the last year, five years, or ten?

Fear of failure	Enthusiasm
Being overwhelmed	Curiosity
Comfortable routine	Boredom
Dread	Drudgery
Excitement	Joy

3. This chapter describes a hopeful hunger for good food: "This hopeful hunger is spiritual; choices I make about eating affect not only my soul but also my local and global neighbors." Is this a new idea

for you? If so, can you see yourself embracing it as you delve into the book? If it is not new for you, how do you resonate with this statement?

4. What prompted you to read this book? How are you hoping to be changed and to think differently about food by the end?

1

The Common Table

Eating . . . is an invitation to enter into communion and be reconciled with each other. To eat with God at the table is to eat with the aim of healing and celebrating the memberships of creation.

—Norman Wirzba[1]

In 2006, our first year back in Newberg, Oregon, after living thirteen years in the Midwest, we built ourselves a house. Mark's mom and stepdad, Donna and Bob, invited us to stay with them so that we could put money toward building a house rather than spending that money on rent. Besides engaging our teaching responsibilities at George Fox University, we (but mostly Mark) spent spare minutes laying floors, doing electrical work, coordinating subcontractors, and building staircases and porches. Nearly every night Mom cooked dinner, insisting that this was her contribution to helping with the house. I say "nearly" because when I could manage it, I cooked Thursday nights, partly because I missed stirring things around in a pot and partly because it seemed right and good to cook our family dinner on a day I had some extra time. On Friday nights Mark and I would often go on a dinner date, usually combined with yet another trip to Home Depot, where we wrestled with choosing light fixtures, water fixtures, and doorknobs. But Mom would have cooked for us seven nights a week if we'd let her.

Around their common table we came to know Bob in ways we hadn't before, and he came to know us. His wry sense of humor made me grimace as much as laugh and reminded me of generational and cultural differences that nevertheless linked us. He had subtle ways of finding out what needed doing and then showing up with the tools to do it. He bestowed gifts like Santa year-round, treasures made or found at Goodwill and then refashioned—like the clothespin basket he made for me after I admired his.

Mom's invitation to her dinner table night after night for a year made room for a friendship to blossom between us and her husband, and our relationship with her plumbed new depths. Maybe witnessing such gracious hospitality got me itching to do more of it myself. Or maybe a deeper truth was ignited: I experienced what God intended eating to accomplish, that is, a grace-filled nourishing that helps us recognize our responsibility for each other's well-being.

We'd never celebrated an equinox before, but since I was itching to be hospitable and since I'd spent a lot of time outdoors that first year back, it was a natural place to begin. When Mark was laying ABS (acrylonitrile butadiene styrene) pipe for downspouts and dealing with vapor barrier and whatnot in the early stages of building, I was hauling bricks, tires, and bottles out of the creek, forging a more certain trail through the woods along the deer path, and pulling up invasive Canadian Thistle, also known as "lettuce from hell." (I am not joking; Canadian Thistle is related to lettuce and is often called by that name.) I noted subtle seasonal changes in Oregon foliage that I'd missed during our thirteen years in the Midwest. I had time to pay attention, which inclined me to stand still and take note. Celebrating the equinox that first fall back in Oregon gave me a chance to share my enthusiasm about all the attention I'd been paying to foliage, shifting sunlight, the activity of squirrels, and God's presence in it all.

So I planned away for this outdoor celebration, though not without a hitch or two since all of our belongings were in a storage unit. On occasion I'd wistfully gaze at boxes and disassembled furniture, more than a bit chagrined at how much I missed my stuff. All of that to say, we had no table on which to celebrate. So I bought a used, "rustic" wooden table advertised on Craigslist, and Mark helped me carry it and the benches down to a clearing in the forest. I bought four sage-green plates at Goodwill and yellowy-orange placemats at the dollar store. Mom loaned me serving dishes and silverware, and I decorated with leaves, twigs, Queen Anne's lace, and blue cornflowers.

Mom also helped me make the feast. She loaned me everything I needed to pull it together, including her time. We worked together assembling a three-cheese spinach lasagna she had made for us some time earlier. The recipe takes a lot of work. It requires cooking up a tomato sauce from fresh tomatoes as well as making a béchamel sauce and a spinach ricotta mixture. It requires boiling lots and lots of lasagna noodles and grating cheese and then assembling it all. We talked as we worked side by side—about house building, children, change, the passage of time. I was very aware that she offered her time as a gift to me, even if she may have been a little perplexed as to why I would go to such lengths to fix a dinner for company when I didn't even have a house to serve it in. But even if she wondered such things, she kept them to herself, being the gracious mother-in-law that she is.

Todd and Karen joined us that first year, friends from those tender years when our daughters played together in preschool. Karen brought pears poached in port. I printed out fall poetry from the internet ("Dear books, safely stored, how I miss you!" I murmured as the printer clicked and hummed and then spit out a few sheets of poetry), and we read poems to each other over dessert. It may have felt a bit contrived, corny even, but everyone graciously played a part. We ate around a common table, closing a gap of a dozen years over the course of a night as we talked of losses and gains, joys and challenges.

That outdoor dinner became the foundation for the annual autumn equinox celebration we've had every year since. Every September on or near the fall equinox, our kitchen becomes the prepping place for a feast inspired by the summer-to-fall transition. Mark and I chop, sauté, roast, and bake squash, eggplant, tomatoes, and apples or pears; we offer food made from our own hands, and friendship, and the ordinary grace found in good food and changing seasons. We invite six or so acquaintances or friends with whom we laugh and talk, eat and drink. Then we meander down to the gazebo (lit with candles in jars hanging on landscape posts that Bob found for us at Goodwill), where we sit around the fire and share stories, poetry, songs, pictures, and artwork inspired by fall. It has become a sacramental meal reminiscent of meals from ages past.

A History of Porridge

Throughout most of history, people depended on each other's contributions to a common table. Survival depended on hunting animals, foraging for seasonal grains, fruits, nuts, mushrooms, and root vegetables, and the skills to turn these raw gleanings into edible food. Eventually hunters and gatherers started keeping flocks and herds and cultivating grains. Those who kept (that is, nurtured, doctored, fed, and protected) animals and tended (planted, watered, weeded, and harvested) grains no longer depended exclusively on gathering and hunting. They could plan when to eat meat and store excess wheat, barley, quinoa, or teff—whatever their regional grain might be. As a result, they could awaken to a reliable breakfast every morning.

In the November 2013 issue of *The Atlantic*, a panel of twelve scientists, entrepreneurs, engineers, and historians of technology each chose twenty-five inventions and ranked them according to their significance for humanity. A team compiled the lists and came up with the fifty greatest

✦ *Food for Thought* ✦ *about Equinoxes and Solstices*

I sometimes ask Mark if he knows whether the moon is waxing or waning. He always says waning, figuring that he will be right at least half the time—which he is. Mostly, my asking has made us both more inclined to notice. For thousands of years various religions (including Christianity) linked religious holidays to lunar cycles, equinoxes, and solstices, recognizing the real impact seasonal shifts have on our lives while simultaneously using them to reinforce beliefs.

All of the Jewish holidays are set according to lunar cycles around the solstices and equinoxes, and so their dates shift, just as the date for Easter shifts for Christians. For instance, the Feast of Booths or Feast of Tabernacles is the first of the High Holy Feasts for Jews and marks the beginning of the New Year. It falls on the first new moon after the autumn equinox. Christians follow the First Ecumenical Council of Nicaea, which determined Easter would always be celebrated following Passover. The date of Easter moves around because Passover is held after the first full moon following the spring equinox. One of the beauties inherent in this choice for Easter (besides its relationship to Passover) that was not lost on the early church is the power in celebrating Life resurrected out of death. Easter happens when there are more hours of day than night, which begins with the breakthroughs since the wheel.[2] Six related to food. I would like to emphasize that *only* six out of fifty related to food.

Archimedes's screw (no. 31) made the list, an invention devised in the third century BC that revolutionized irrigation, allowing water to be drawn from canals and streams to irrigate fields. The moldboard plow (no. 30) of the eighteenth century not only dug up soil but turned it over so that hard ground could be cultivated, which (like the screw) expanded farming possibilities. Nitrogen fixation (no. 11) emerged in 1918 and gave us synthetic fertilizer, which aided the so-called green revolution (no. 22) in the mid-twentieth century[3]—which, when combined with scientific plant breeding (no. 38), increased the amount of food we could pull out of every

spring equinox. In the early church, solstices and equinoxes landed on the twenty-fifth of the month rather than the twenty-first. Since Christmas was given an actual date, it was not moved even after the calendar shifted. Our observance of Jesus's birth on the longest night of the year (the winter solstice) underscores the significance of the Light from Heaven breaking into our darkness.

> Because of God's tender mercy,
>   the morning light from heaven is about to break upon us,
> to give light to those who sit in darkness and in the shadow of
>   death,
>   and to guide us to the path of peace.
>
> Luke 1:78–79

Linking religious celebrations to equinoxes and solstices reflects a deep connection and respect for Earth's seasons and cycles.

Once we traded mostly outdoor lives for mostly indoor ones and stopped growing our own food, we no longer had much need or reason to pay attention to seasonal cycles. We didn't see the moon enough to know whether it was waxing toward full or waning toward new; we didn't mark the first day of autumn, winter, spring, or summer. Might redeeming these days by using them to celebrate the cyclical pattern of God's predictable, wonderful, and amazing creation be a kind of worship?

acre of farmland. And finally, the combine harvester (no. 50), invented in the 1930s, made it possible for one person to do the job of a whole slew of field laborers.

Farmer/writers such as Wendell Berry and Wes Jackson, founder of The Land Institute, argue for putting the plow at or near the top of the list of monumental change agents. DNA researcher and social history writer Alistair Moffat states that "the great invention, the greatest revolution in our history was the invention of farming." Most agrarian philosophers, historians, and activists would likely agree. Furthermore, Moffat asserts that farming changed the world because of the invention of porridge.[4]

Not many would quibble over a claim that farming changed the course of history, but porridge? Moffat takes the story back to the emergence of a reliable source of grain. People stopped tracking their food across the continent and settled in. They gathered for common meals over open fires and stewing pots, fires they could keep burning since they no longer needed to be nomadic to survive. Porridges, stews, and mutton cooked on spits brought people together to eat as part of a daily rhythm of sustenance, giving and receiving from each other as they fed their bodies, rested, and—perhaps most important—reinforced strong bonds with those with whom they lived and worked.

Using the energy that formerly went toward hunting and gathering, they crafted civilizations by building fortresses. With a stable food supply that could be turned into mush, mothers could feed their babies something besides breast milk (Moffat's big argument). As a result, they weaned babies earlier and therefore had more children, which grew the human population substantially, adding people power that brought about all kinds of inventions and social changes.

Some of these changes made the world a better place, or at least a more comfortable and convenient place for people. Some did not. The agricultural trajectory worked out better for humans than for the rest of creation. Not surprisingly, some unintended consequences of change that seemed good at the time have now come back to haunt humans, who depend on a whole and healthy creation for their own well-being. Theologian Norman Wirzba, quoted at the beginning of this chapter, is right to suggest that eating is an invitation to celebration as well as reconciliation and healing.

Grain that has been cracked, rolled, cut, or crushed and then cooked in water is still a worldwide breakfast. It says something powerful about the staying power of real food, that is, whole foods that have not been overly tampered with, processed, added to, or subtracted from. Eating a hearty, steaming bowl of rolled oats dips our spoons, as it were, into an ever-simmering pot of porridge, linking us to a past that offers some guidance toward healing and reconciling eating habits that went awry. Oats make for a humble breakfast, and humility is a good first step.

Until the Industrial Revolution, farming (and eating) practices changed slowly. Roman plows and early American plows looked and worked pretty much the same. The ox- or horse-drawn plow aided hand plows for those who could afford oxen or horses, but otherwise the planting, cultivating, harvesting, and winnowing of grain went on relatively unchanged.

That an agricultural revolution would tag along behind the Industrial Revolution as new tools and practices replaced traditional ones makes all kinds of sense. Like the Industrial Revolution, the agricultural revolution that followed changed us in profound ways, particularly our relationship with food: how we grow it, yes, but also how we cook it, what we think about it, and how we eat it.

For example, the Industrial Revolution shifted labor away from farms to other places of employment. People commuted to work in factories and later to banks, schools, hospitals, libraries, stores, hotels, restaurants, and Wall Street. In 1790 (near the beginning of the Industrial Revolution), 90 percent of US laborers worked on farms. By 1900 that number had dropped to 38 percent. In 2010 less than 1 percent of the population claimed farming as an occupation, and about 2 percent of the population lived on farms.

To accommodate men who left home to commute to work elsewhere (as well as women and children in the lower classes), the main meal shifted from a big meal generally eaten together in the middle of the day to dinner at the end of the day, which was also usually eaten together. By the nineteenth century, families had figured out how to transport food for a midday meal in containers that would keep the lunches clean and safe from the various hazards of the working factory. The earliest lunch pails were woven baskets, which were eventually replaced with tobacco tins refashioned with handles to accommodate leftovers, hard-boiled eggs, bread and cheese, or sandwiches wrapped in a kerchief for a quick midday meal that was eaten alone or with coworkers. By the 1930s schoolchildren started sporting lunch boxes, and by the 1950s, when consumption came to define the post-WWII self, lunch boxes became a marketable item and an important back-to-school supply.

From Lunch Pail to Pop-Tarts

In the last fifty years we've grown increasingly accustomed to eating away from home, away from anything resembling a common table. In *Cooked*, Michael Pollan tells the anthropological story of the communal power of the cook fire that helped form us as social beings. In his brief social history of fire, he describes our movement from communal to isolated eating. First, Pollan says, we tamed fire and became social creatures who gathered, cooked, and ate around it. Then we brought fire inside with stone fireplaces, and then we made cast-iron ovens that eventually were replaced by steel ones. Soon after, fire disappeared altogether from our cooking, replaced by invisible electric currents running through ovens and radio waves bouncing off glass and plastic in our microwaves. By then we had pretty much left off cooking and eating with clan or family and popped frozen burritos in the microwave, eating on our own. Pollan concludes, "The microwave is as antisocial as the cook fire is communal."[5]

Not surprisingly, a variety of studies support that we have become increasingly antisocial—more accurately asocial or isolated—in our eating patterns. Hearty, steaming bowls of porridge eaten to shore up energy for the day have been replaced by anything that can be consumed in a rush at the break of day—like a Pop-Tart (cinnamon brown sugar!) eaten on the way to the bus stop.

Post, the cereal company, created the first Pop-Tart-like food more than fifty years ago. In 1963 they rolled out the Country Square. This single-serving breakfast substitute (which doubled as an after-school snack) didn't need refrigeration, which was a big selling point. Kellogg stole the market six months later with Pop-Tarts, and while a lot of similar products fill grocery store shelves now, the multinational company sells millions of Pop-Tarts each year to families on the run. In fact, Pop-Tarts are so well favored that the US military airdropped 2.4 million of them into Afghanistan during the US invasion.[6]

Families in the United States live in a culture that still values families eating together. We see it in news articles, journal articles, and books about families. We see family dinners depicted in television series that include comedy (*Modern Family*), family drama (*Parenthood*), historical drama (*Downton Abbey*), reality television (*Duck Dynasty*), and even law-and-order shows (*Blue Bloods*). Our norms suggest that eating meals on the run ought to be the *exception* to the rule rather than the rule. Still, this exception became less, well, *exceptional* as a necessary adaptation to facilitate afternoon and evening activities for parents and children alike.

Commercials, on the other hand, suggest that we are mostly a culture that eats fast food—that is, food on the run or food-for-fuel. Large food corporations producing those commercials are glad to meet America's need for "nutritional" on-the-go food.

Food norms reflect a culture's values and beliefs, and the United States is a culture without consensus on these matters. We are young, after all—only 250 years old. Historically speaking, the United States was the great experiment that (theoretically) welcomed people from all national backgrounds, converging to form one great nation and blending the strengths of the countries from which we came. But we've come to realize that's not who we are. The United States is a country striving not only to value the differences represented among us but also to become better for having them. We work, with much difficulty, to foster rather than blur distinctions. While I prefer that goal, it probably means we will always be prone to food fads and swayed by a market eager both to fill the void of a food culture and to define our wants and needs for us.

In part, we long for something akin to a family dinner. However, we have a fairly firmly entrenched cultural belief that work, sports, music, drama, and various other civic and church-related opportunities offer more self-fulfillment and personal development than a family-cooked dinner enjoyed at leisure with the entire family—and maybe a guest or three or four—gathered around a table.

Communion

Here's a trivia question: What has changed the most in the last fifty years—the number of family meals eaten together or what family members do besides eat when they sit down together for supper? Regarding the first part of that question, nutritionist Katherine Brooking cites a study in a medical journal that found that 43 percent of American families eat together daily, while a *CBS News* poll found that 75 percent of viewers said their families eat together daily.[7] That discrepancy goes to show that survey results depend somewhat on who gets asked. I can imagine that parents and teenagers might tally up family dinners differently.

Brooking also notes that even if we sit down together to eat somewhat *regularly* (a term she intentionally leaves vague), we don't engage each other as much. Besides eating, it appears that for a third of the CBS viewers the television is always on during mealtime, and nearly another third said it's on half the time. For some, the television provides background noise; for others it's a substitute for conversation. What's more, since we are seldom separated from our phones, is it any wonder that engaging our phones is becoming part of mealtime? One in ten folks in the CBS poll said that at least some of the time family members use their phones to text friends to set up after-dinner plans, follow the Blazers game, play games, or answer email during dinner. I wonder how long it will be before I get a text during a Thanksgiving dinner from someone sitting next to me that says, "hey pass the potatoes plz."

Jason Mitchell's doctoral dissertation provides a review of the research outlining benefits linked with families that eat together.[8] Developmental and behavioral problems in children are fewer, and families tend to communicate and support each other better. Likewise, children do better both academically and socially and are less likely to abuse drugs and alcohol or to suffer from depression. Mitchell notes that these studies are correlational—that is, families that eat together tend to be socially and physically healthier. That doesn't mean that eating together *makes* families socially or physically healthier. I remember an audacious claim I read a number of years ago: eat dinner together, and your teenage daughter will not get pregnant.

The oversimplification annoyed me then, and it annoys me still. Families that eat together are still plagued with conflict, tension, and troubles, and families that don't eat together raise children who grow up well-adjusted—without teen pregnancies, addictions, depression, or school dropout issues.

But still, what if eating together makes a difference in the social, emotional, and physical well-being of family members?

Perhaps the findings are about something else—something that doesn't get measured in studies. Perhaps we are discussing a value as old as humanity itself, a value that is necessary for health and well-being—a core value of Christian faith. What if the findings are about the value of communion, the acceptance of the belief that we belong to something bigger than our isolated selves? Communion recognizes that we are members of communities that lay some claim on our choices, but communion is also life affirming. Wirzba links this value to Christian faith when he says that "trinitarian-inspired eating means that we eat to share and nurture life. . . . [I]t is about extending hospitality and making room for others to find life by sharing in our own. Self-offering, accepting responsibility for another's well-being, turning one's own life into nurture for others—these are the signs of life as empowered by the Spirit."⁹

Studies that show links between eating together and well-being are telling us something important, even if a theologically grounded purpose for eating together is missing. Perhaps the findings in these studies reflect a grace-filled truth that joining with others over food offers a kind of scaffolding, a support to negotiate the trials of living in a postmodern, post-industrial, consumer-driven, individualistic culture.

In her book, *Eat with Joy*, Rachel Marie Stone says that things happen around the table that can't happen elsewhere. "Perhaps more than anything, it's the place where children absorb the message: *These are my people, and I belong here*."¹⁰ Eating with others gives us the daily opportunity to engage ideas, troubleshoot conflicts, encourage, inspire, correct, love, and be loved—both in body and soul.

I fear that sounds simplistic. I will attempt to clarify.

Communion, Take Two: The Attentive, Compassionate, Grateful Table

"Here I am! I stand at the door and knock. If anyone hears my voice and opens the door, I will come in and eat with him and he with me." I memorized Revelation 3:20 in third grade, probably for Pioneer Girls. I heard sermons about opening my heart's door to Jesus and liked the paintings of Jesus standing in warm yellow lamplight, knocking on a wooden door. What I *don't* remember is hearing much about the eating part.

While references to eating are sprinkled throughout the Bible like a solid dusting of powdered sugar over French toast, until recently I mostly missed them, and I doubt I'm the only one. My food has pretty much always been guaranteed, so food and eating references felt inconsequential for the most part; the main point was to get our souls in order. However, for those for whom food is not guaranteed, identifying with stories of harvests, feasts, sacrifices, drought, famine, and farming is more natural. Only recently have I come to see the deeply spiritual nature of food—physical, fragrant, savory food.

As it turns out, food is both a pleasure and our salvation. We need to eat to live, and either a plant or an animal needs to die so that we can go on living. But Jesus also sustains life now, not just because of what he did in the past but because he holds all creation together (Col. 1:17). Jesus comes to us, knocks on the door, and sits down for a meal—maybe spinach salad with hazelnuts, cranberries, and feta; butternut squash ravioli with pine nuts and sage browned butter; and apple strudel for dessert.

Feeding his disciples was one of the first things Jesus did after the resurrection—a breakfast of roasted fish served on the seashore by the risen Rabbi.

Eating offers a pleasurable way of communing. Unlike our family cat, Pollifax, whose diet consists of raw field mice and dry cat food eaten alone (generally with efficient gusto), eating isn't simply a functional pleasure. We are created with potential to enter each other's lives as we break bread together, to give and receive and enjoy pleasure as we partake in food that keeps us alive. The mystery of communion is that we eat in order to live more fully. We eat with others, with Jesus in our midst, that we might live better, love better, and be grateful.

When Protestants speak of communion, they typically mean a ceremony where bread and wine (or grape juice) are eaten and sipped to remember Christ, who sacrificed all for us. Various traditions practice communion in different ways and emphasize different elements and purposes.[11] My own religious tribe, the Quakers, observes the sacrament of communion during quiet communal worship every Sunday rather than with elements. We work to see all moments of life as sacramental—every meal as sacred time, an encounter with God. As an observant Quaker I fail at this; every meal does not, in fact, feel like communion.

It comforts me to remember that the possibility of sharing communion with God at each meal takes place more through God's initiation than through my ability to make it happen. Therefore I embrace the practice, however feebly, because I want to be engulfed daily in God's love and presence, mindful of my commitments and belongingness, my shortcomings and need for reconciliation. When I pay attention, I more easily remember that life is sustained by God's daily grace and the sacrifices that bring me food.

Communion painted in broader strokes depicts a close relationship with another or others—a membership, as Wendell Berry and Norman Wirzba are fond of saying, a fondness that has rubbed off on me. Eating toward communion is to acknowledge various memberships: that we belong to God and are members of the human race, yes, but also that we share the earth with animals, plants, and microbes. All of earth's members depend on being able to sup from a global table that offers good water, clean air, and fertile soil chock-full of life. Wirzba says, "To know and appreciate these memberships, *and then to live sympathetically and compassionately into them*, is the crucial task."[12]

Jesus directed his followers to gather with thankfulness, to remember God's faithfulness, and to give and receive daily graces to and from each other. This is a reminder that we do not live independently of others but are sustained by the sacrifice and work of plants and animals, as well as the sacrifice and work of farm and ranch laborers, butchers and bakers, shelf stockers, and cashiers.

To challenge notions of autonomy and independence, I ask the college students in my Introduction to Sociology class whether they think they can make a hamburger without anyone else's help. On the first pass they say yes. Even if they've not done much in the way of cooking, they are pretty sure they can figure it out. I imagine they take access to YouTube videos for granted, though they couldn't go online if they were making a hamburger without help.

I ask them where they would get the cow, and suddenly we are having a very different conversation. "Without help" means they have to acquire a cow (ideally without stealing it), kill it, skin it, butcher it, create a way to grind the meat into hamburger, make a fire, and figure out something to use as a pan or grill to cook it on. Assuming they want a bun, they have to find, harvest, and grind their own wheat, discover the mysteries of yeast, and craft some sort of oven to bake it in. If they want onion, ketchup, mustard, and pickles (not to mention bacon!), each of these ingredients (except perhaps the onion) presents a challenge. By this time in our discussion, they decide they will settle for a skewered hunk of flesh cooked over an open flame, but they realize even this is not as simple as they initially thought.

Embracing rather than fighting interdependence fosters humility, and really, neediness is not so bad. We need people who will work in fields and care for, slaughter, and butcher animals. We need grass for cows to eat, insects to pollinate fruits and vegetables, healthy soil to support pasture, forests, orchards, and plants of all sorts. We need good water and clean air. All at once, we see that we are members of something far bigger than the human race.

Once I recognized my interdependence and membership within larger communities, sympathy started percolating in the core of my being, inclining me toward compassion. Mark and I have become part of a growing number of people looking for ways to get food grown or raised in compassionate ways. We want workers to be paid a livable wage, animals to be raised humanely, and the soil to be treated in ways that foster its health—even if that makes it more difficult to control pests and weeds and to grow giant brussels sprouts.

Perhaps what this compassion and longing for justice is really about, as Wirzba suggests, is a desire to reconcile with God's divine love, which envelops all of God's creation. This integrated body-soul mindfulness gives full expression to the reconciling work of Jesus. By partaking in the sacrament of communion, we take Jesus into our mouths and bodies, a physical reminder that Jesus offers life and grace through his blood and body.

Theoretically, I can eat mindfully when I am alone, but I find it easier to be mindful when I am eating with another. Food that I grab from Subway and consume mindlessly to fill gut hunger while driving hither and yon is the opposite of communion. When I partake alone, I more easily stay blissfully ignorant of connections to my food and of memberships that call me toward empathy and compassion for all the people, animals, insects, and fire-water-air elements of creation that contributed something to the filling of my stomach.

Stretching toward Communion

Most of us conform a fair bit to the norms of our culture; we can't help it—norm conformity helps us fit into a community. As a result, most of us twenty-first-century Westerners struggle to balance norms that demand a high level of commitment to work and activities we value for ourselves and our children with a desire for communion and opportunities to forge bonds over food with our family and friends.

However, any and all of us can accept the invitation to eat at a common table by being more intentional about what we are eating, more attentive to those who share our table, and more grateful for God, others, and God's creation that sustains us. We move toward *intention* when we do some sleuthing and then make informed and life-giving choices about food we purchase (more on this to come). We move toward *attention* when we slow down, value, and engage those in whose presence we are eating. We move toward *gratitude* through the simple discipline of saying grace before a meal and saying thank you afterward.

Being intentional is being neighborly—an outward expression of our faith. It can mean committing to eating only fair-trade chocolate or going without it; it can mean buying eggs produced by pasture-based hens or going without them. Being intentional means learning the true cost of food and then choosing compassion and justice over convenience or thrift. Being intentional is also about thinking beyond what we eat as individuals to the eating needs of others. I'm not as good at this practice, but I want to stretch toward reflecting what the church has embraced since the beginning: feeding the hungry, eating with the lonely, and taking food to families with new babies or who may be dealing with illness, death, or grief.

My mother used candles to move us toward attentiveness. As a U-2 pilot for the Air Force, my father had an erratic schedule. He spent three to six months away any given year, and often when he was home his flight schedule required him to go to bed early and leave before dawn. On days we ate dinner together, my mother wanted her four young children to be calm, so sometimes she lit candles. The gently flickering flames brought us to a kind of awed attention, and this simple gesture did calm us. Candles made it easier for me to resist the temptation to poke Dan in the ribs to make him spit out his food (and get in trouble) or for Dan to make faces at Kathy to make her laugh so she'd spew food across the table (and get in trouble). The more peaceful atmosphere helped us refrain from feeding our dog, Dragon Lady (the nickname for the type of plane Dad flew), under the table. We'd offer her tidbits and then compete for bragging rights about who was her favorite. All of these behaviors elicited a sharp reprimand from our mother when Dad was absent. While a look from Dad would still us equally well, candles made paying attention *nice*. I remember candlelit dinners and a kind of gentle communion that transpired those nights. We *tasted* our food rather than inhaled it. We talked, but mostly, we children learned to listen, which nourished our bodies and our relationships.

Others can move us toward attention—as my mother attempted to do with candles—or we can help others. When Mark and I first moved to the Midwest, our youngest daughter had a hard time transitioning, as we all did in our various ways. That first year I was home preparing for comprehensive exams and writing my dissertation proposal, and I did what I could to ease the transition for our daughters. About once a week I'd pick up Megan Anna from school for lunch and bring her home to a table set with placemats from my Granny—pink gingham rectangles with little white napkins hand painted with ducks. We'd eat simple food, sandwiches mostly, or Megan Anna's favorite, macaroni and cheese, on the Desert Rose dishes I acquired from my mother. I don't remember what we talked about—maybe our dreams from the night before or school or Oregon or projects or friends or the lack thereof. Then I'd take her back to school, both of us a little heartbroken at her sadness, yet hopeful, wanting to believe our connection in the middle of the day gave her a bit of strength and boldness and courage to keep trying to make friends, to fit in, to be okay with our choice to move her so far away from home.

Moving toward attention and strengthening relationships with friends and family is not always a sober task. We stretch toward communion when we go hog wild with a party. All that is required is a few friends, an idea or two, a bit of time shifted away from some other discretionary activity, and a measure of grace to fill in the gaps.

Eating dinner in a fort made of blankets in the living room creates memories and forges bonds of trust that are woven through love and laughter. Hosting themed parties—vintage night, game night, murder mysteries, pumpkin-carving parties, hoity-toity parties, and equinox and solstice celebrations—introduces laughter (which is something most of us could use a lot more of) and deepens friendships and memberships.

Picnics take food back to its origins. Eating outside in the sunlight, with fresh flowers and the occasional yellow jacket looking for a treat, surely calls forth gratitude (except for maybe the yellow jacket—though knowing they feast on insects that feast on our garden helps me tolerate them). Ordinary sandwiches, carrot sticks, roasted nuts, apples, and a bit of chocolate taste more crisp, sweet, and rich when eaten midway through a hike while overlooking a waterfall or the ocean or a forest glade. It is as though our dependence on food, on others, on the earth, and on God is laid bare when we eat in creation's company.

The discipline of saying grace moves us upward toward gratitude, as does the simple act of acknowledging and thanking those who have contributed to feeding us. Mark and I often ask God's blessing on farmers, bakers, bees, and our chickens as a way of offering thanks to invisible or nonhuman sacrifices and work rendered. Sometimes we recite this simple, traditional blessing together: "Dear God, bless these gifts to our use, and us to Your service, and keep us ever mindful of the needs of others." Saying grace reminds us that food is a physical grace that keeps us going day after day.

For the most part, this has been a chapter about eating with others, but meals eaten alone can be eaten with a mindfulness of God's sustaining presence in our food and an awareness of our connection to others. We are never, after all, really alone. Besides, God knocks at the door, wanting to come in and eat with us.

When the weather allows it and I can wrestle myself out of the complacency that tells me eating alone at the kitchen table is more sane and easier than eating lunch outside, I take my plate up to the tree house or out to a rocking chair on the porch. Eating outside stops me from multitasking (checking email over lunch, for instance), which helps me to eat in God's presence more fully, to be aware of the world more fully, and to accept God's invitation to sup—to sit beside me, drawing me into communion with all God is and loves.

• *Shiitake Mushroom and Roasted Pepper Penne* •

8 oz.	penne or fettuccine pasta
2 tbsp.	olive oil or butter (or better yet, a combination)
2 c.	(or more) shiitake mushrooms (other hearty mushrooms such

	as portabello, chanterelle, or whatever is native to your area can be substituted)
½ c.	fresh basil
1 c.	(or more) fresh spinach
1 tbsp.	lemon juice
2–3	cloves garlic
⅓ c.	roasted or smoked sweet peppers (roasted tomatoes can be substituted for a different, but equally delectable, taste)
½ c.	Parmesan cheese
⅓–½ c.	half-and-half or heavy cream
1 tbsp.	pine nuts, toasted (optional)

Start a kettle of lightly salted water for boiling the pasta. Mince garlic, slice shiitake mushroom caps, thinly slice basil, and chop spinach. Add the pasta to the water and cook as directed (8–11 minutes).

Meanwhile, on low heat, heat the 2 tablespoons oil or butter in a skillet and add garlic. Sauté until soft but not browned. Add the mushrooms, turn the heat up to medium, and cook for 4–5 minutes until the mushrooms are soft. Turn off the heat and stir in chopped spinach, basil, lemon juice, and salt and pepper to taste. Cover the skillet and set aside.

Grate ½ cup Parmesan cheese and chop smoked peppers. Once the pasta is done, drain and add to the skillet along with peppers, half-and-half, and ⅔ of the cheese. Stir to combine and serve immediately, garnishing with more fresh basil, the remaining cheese, and pine nuts.

Reflections and Questions

1. Was a common table ever a part of your home? If so, describe it. If not, did you share that experience in the homes of others? What memories do you have of eating around a dinner table, either for holidays or during ordinary times?

2. How do you note the changing seasons in your home in both small and big ways? Can you imagine how acknowledging seasonal shifts might make it easier to see the presence of God in your kitchen and around your table? If this is a new concept, what might it look like

for you to note changing seasons with a growing awareness of God's presence in the shifts and changes throughout the year?

3. How many of your meals are of the microwave/on-the-go/solitary variety, and how many fit into the cook-and-eat-it-with-others/communal category? What would it take to plan one extra meal of the cook-and-eat-with-others variety this week?

4. What does the picture of a pot of porridge (or oatmeal) conjure up for you? Maybe a warm fire on a snowy day? Being forced to eat tasteless mush as a child? What were the breakfast foods of your childhood, and do you still eat them? If you don't, why did you change? Was it a change for better or worse, and how so?

5. Does this chapter (and the last two questions) incline you to feel guilty for eating or serving Pop-Tarts, macaroni and cheese from a box, and microwavable dinners from time to time? Since guilt is never a good motivator, it might be helpful to reflect on the good news, that is, the grace of God news, for facing guilt in the light of various values you hold. Reflect on or talk about discrepancies you experience between differing personal, family, and ecological health goals, values, and needs. Take time to think about and then consider one thing you can change now to lessen the discrepancy. What else might you change in six months? A year?

6. Earlier in this chapter, Wirzba says: "Trinitarian-inspired eating means that we eat to share and nurture life. . . . [I]t is about extending hospitality and making room for others to find life by sharing in our own. Self-offering, accepting responsibility for another's well-being, turning one's own life into nurture for others—these are the signs of life as empowered by the Spirit." Sit with this challenging picture of eating. How does it speak to your various obligations and memberships? How daunting is it? How empowering? Can you find inspiration and encouragement in ways you do this already? Journal or share your thoughts.

7. Read John 21:1–14 and reflect on this story of Jesus eating with his disciples on the beach shortly after he had been crucified. Why might Jesus have chosen to fix the disciples breakfast instead of teaching, reprimanding, or instructing them? Imagine, for a minute, what it would be like to eat with Jesus. How might it change what it means

to eat when doing so with the One who called all things into being, including the very food you are eating?

8. How do you practice the sacrament of communion? What does reading about communion as discussed in this chapter add to how you might deepen your experience of it?

9. This chapter mentions that "being intentional [about what one eats] is being neighborly—an outward expression of our faith." What would it take to learn the hidden cost of a food you eat regularly and then to make a commitment (small or large) to eating that food more ethically this month?

2
Cooking
Artful Transformations

He who works with his hands is a laborer. He who works with his hands and his head is a craftsman. He who works with his hands and his head and his heart is an artist.

—often attributed to Francis of Assisi

Fern Creek is my home, the five acres we live on outside Newberg, Oregon. Most of it is forest and home to many other creatures, and from about an acre and a half we feed one hundred people fruits and vegetables from our community supported agriculture (CSA) farm. Last November, Fern Creek's kitchen filled with folks who came together to make holiday hors d'oeuvres. Aromas from sautéing onions, pan-frying potato cakes, and spinach and cheese pastries wafted through the room. November's chill disappeared as we were warmed by a heated oven, steam rising from the pots on the stovetop, and the good cheer that follows laughter.

The summer before, Terrie, a culinary expert and member of our CSA, picked up her crate of produce like a child anticipating birthday presents. "Oh!" she'd exclaim, "these onions are beautiful!" and "Oh! The corn . . . and beautiful tomatoes! And delicata squash—I love cooking with delicata squash!" Her exuberance matched mine. All that exuberance led to conversations about cooking and food, and *that* led to an idea.

Now we cook together. Occasionally it's just the two of us experimenting with recipes or decorating ornate Christmas cookies. But usually it's with others for a Fern Creek Community Cooking Class. Our idea was to invite people into our exuberance.

Usually we plan a seasonal menu for our classes (butternut ravioli with sage browned butter sauce in October, a variety of soups and complementing breads in January), but in November we planned a sparkly menu from around the world. Chicken satay with spicy peanut sauce from Southeast Asia, vegetarian dolmas from the Middle East, spanakopita from Greece,

Scandinavian lox and cucumber canapes, celeriac potato latkes with apple-onion compote (a traditional European and Middle Eastern dish), and a spicy bean dip using Jacob's Cattle beans from Fern Creek. We finished the evening with classic shortbread and hot buttered rum, eaten around a table set to celebrate autumn.

Six people join Terrie and me for each class, which is mostly attended by women. We generally have a man or two as well, and they are as capable and interested in rolling out freshly made pasta for ravioli or chopping carrots and onions as anyone else. Sometimes people sign up alone; sometimes they sign up with a daughter or mother or friend or spouse. Folks of all sorts come to learn new ways to work wonders in the kitchen. Terrie, who tosses words like *brunois* and *chiffonaide* and *Beurre Noisette* around as though French is her native tongue, teaches us proper ways to dice and "sweat" vegetables, as well as how to make fresh pasta, wontons, strudel, and meat stock.

People seem to want opportunities to cook. More specifically, people are drawn into a creative process that encourages thinking differently about cooking. We are often inspired in the homes of friends, and Terrie and I hope our classes feel like that—an opportunity to be inspired while making a mess in someone else's kitchen. With the planning and shopping already done, people can simply cook, eat, and clean up together; our hope is that unhelpful comparisons and fears of not measuring up fall away.

Even folks not particularly drawn to the kitchen—those who might use the word *drudgery* when describing their relationship with pots and pans—say that our classes are fun. More than that, they find it satisfying to connect and engage with others around a task that is as old as time. What we are primarily doing is taking a job often done alone at the end of a harried day and infusing it with enthusiasm, companionship, and artistry.

Not that every cooking experience could be, or should be, experienced in this way. But like any communal celebration, Fern Creek Community Cooking Classes remind us who gather in the kitchen that cooking can be an artistic expression of nourishing affection. Still, cooking nourishes affection whether or not it feels particularly artistic—whether it is done alone for oneself, alone for oneself and others, or in the company of others for others. The sacrifice of time in the kitchen is a daily reminder of God's sustaining grace as evidenced in the food we prepare and eat.

Israel's communal celebrations reminded people of God's presence, protection, delivery from slavery, forgiveness, and sustaining love, which they experienced through good harvests and nourishing rain. Joy-infused festivals and feasts helped them stay mindful about things they might forget, that they might start taking for granted. Certainly the preparation for such feasts would have been enormous, and it was likely done in community. I imagine laughing, storytelling, and life-sharing between women and girls as well as men and boys as they readied the feast—grinding meal and baking bread, slaughtering and dressing the lamb, cutting and boiling vegetables, gathering fruit and nuts, and preparing the wine.

To the Israelites and to our ancestors across time and cultures, much of the ordinary, daily work of cooking surely felt like a chore. Some of that comes with most any repetitive labor. Even with the conveniences of indoor plumbing, refrigeration, and grocery stores, cooks in twenty-first-century kitchens still describe cooking (at least occasionally) as wearisome.

When I feel weary of cooking, having to decide what to cook becomes taxing in and of itself. I can stand in front of my well-stocked pantry and feel stymied, bored with my options, uninspired, and unmotivated.

I know I'm not alone in this.

The default for our middle-class culture seems to be pizza. Collective eating patterns in the twenty-first century include a lot of eating out (Pizza Hut anyone?), ordering takeout (Domino's?), bringing home "almost" homemade options and cooking them ourselves (Papa Murphy's), and/or baking or microwaving frozen food (like DiGiorno).

However, the drudgery surrounding cooking is not only a result of having to do it day after day. There's a mountain of money to be made by food corporations eager to take the load off our shoulders. The need to find or create consumers for processed, ready-to-eat meals dovetailed nicely with women's changing roles during the twentieth century.

Food Economics 101: From Village to Supermarket

Picture a small town in the early 1900s, nestled in a valley. Imagine some of the hills forested, some speckled with sheep and cows, and some plowed and planted in rows of crops. The spire of a church steeple rises above low-lying fog. A bakery or two, a butcher shop, a dressmaker's shop, a general store, a doctor's office, and a post office line the main boulevard. A few inns and pubs (pubs being more idyllic than saloons) are scattered throughout town. A one-room schoolhouse and a blacksmith or tool repair shop are nestled somewhere in the scene as well.

The food eaten by the inhabitants of such a village comes primarily from the surrounding farms and from their own family gardens, which supply them with summer crops and root vegetables preserved or stored throughout the year.

When people needed a dress or a hat, a hammer or nails, they bought it from their neighbor, as it were, who sold such items for their livelihood. Some items were imported—fabric, sugar, coffee, windows, lamps, and most of the non-food items in the general store—but by and large, small towns were local economies, meaning that most of the money and goods that exchanged hands between people who lived in the same communities stayed in that community. People supported each other by purchasing each other's services and goods. Neighborly affection, at least in terms of mutual economic support, abounded.

Yes, some products in those 1900s towns arrived by trains and wagons from faraway places, but not many of them. Exporting and importing had been around a good while at that point in history—cinnamon, paprika, and raisins had traveled by camel across deserts for several thousand years already. International trade revved up significantly in the seventeenth century with Europe's race to explore and colonize major parts of the world, claiming those places as their own and bringing home treasures found abroad. Then a chain of events morphed local economies into a nearly global one. It started with the Industrial Revolution, which culminated in a burst of activity during and just following WWII, and was followed by an explosion of international commerce in the 1970s, as many local corporations became multinational enterprises.

These events changed many things, including the way we eat.

WWI and WWII provided much of the impetus and motivation to develop processed food. Throughout history, feeding troops has been one of an army's great challenges. By the turn of the twentieth century, food was being processed and packaged in cans and tins, and the wartime use of these foods increased the drive to produce them. Dependable supplies of canned corned beef, sardines, hard bread, dehydrated potatoes, baked beans, and coffee made it easier for soldiers on the move to eat well—or well enough.

After WWI, the food industry continued to work with the military to figure out better ways to feed soldiers. The military wanted a variety of foods that would taste good, food that might remind soldiers of home and help boost morale as well as keep them well nourished. By the time the United States entered WWII, field rations had become part of the solution, and the program (which is still in use today) continued to evolve during and after the war. Rations provided a complete meal-in-a-can or package: beef stews, beef with noodles, or lamb stew packaged along with chocolate, coffee, and sugar. The creation of a 600-calorie, high-protein, high-fat bar worked well for troops marching across Europe.[1]

On the home front, "rations" had a different meaning altogether. To supply the war effort, Great Britain and the United States introduced a rationing system, limiting how much of certain items civilians back home could buy. Rationed items included foods like sugar, coffee, cheese, meat, and canned goods, as well as tires, cars, bicycles, shoes, typewriters, women's nylons, and gasoline. All cars deemed nonessential, which constituted about half of them, were allowed four gallons a week. Great Britain and the United States encouraged citizens to plant "victory gardens" as a way to contribute to the war effort; by growing their own vegetables and fruits, the people at home could free up other food resources for soldiers abroad.

Imagine *any* of that today. It's difficult, nearly unimaginable. Not that I'd actually wish for it, but I can't help wondering whether something akin to rationing might curb our twenty-first-century appetite for stuff, including easy food.

At any rate, after the war the citizenry was well rewarded for their sacrifices. The food industry that fed soldiers turned its marketing eye to civilians. Industries of all kinds expanded into new postwar markets. Science had made breakthroughs in converting petroleum to plastics, chemicals, and cosmetics, and more was known about communications that used radio waves and televised images. Economic growth and optimism following WWI and WWII offered a fertile ground for industrial capitalism to come into fullness on a multitude of fronts.

The homemaker became the best new consumer of prepackaged, precooked, ready-to-eat meals. Products such as Kellogg's cereals, SpaghettiOs, Kraft Macaroni & Cheese, and Spam seemed endless, and British and American housewives embraced them enthusiastically. Coming off a time of scarcity, uncertainty, and hard work, the processed foods were miracles of abundance and embracing them a marker of victory, progress, and family and national health.

I don't fault my mother's generation for seeing Hamburger Helper as a welcome aid in the kitchen. Beyond its convenience, I imagine some women bought such products out of pride in a country that emerged victorious from hard-fought wars that had cost people much.

Food Economics 201: A Changing Image in the Kitchen

Betty Crocker was invented in the 1920s to sell cake and bread mixes, but she became iconic as an advice-giving guru who inspired women to see housekeeping and cooking as honorable and satisfying callings. Susan Marks, author of *Finding Betty Crocker: The Secret Life of America's First Lady of Food*, unpacks this history and briefly discusses Betty Crocker's role in shifting the American diet from whole foods to factory-processed convenience foods.

But it wasn't just Betty Crocker mixes that changed cooking. Frozen TV dinners arrived in grocery stores in the early 1950s. Swanson executive Gerry Thomas saw his first three-compartment aluminum tray on a Pan Am Airways flight and is credited with bringing these prepackaged frozen meals into the American home. The first came out in 1952, but the boom came the next year following a turkey surplus after Thanksgiving. What to do with leftover turkey? Make leftovers! The first Swanson TV dinners included turkey with cornbread dressing, potatoes, and frozen peas; more than 10 million dinners were sold in the United States, the population of which was about 150 million at the time. The rest, as they say, is history.

In spite of Betty Crocker's efforts to the contrary, prepackaged processed foods offered convenience that melded with other social forces, so that by the 1950s the American diet had pretty well shifted, along with a dominant view that drudgery best defined cooking in the same way that it defined washing diapers and scrubbing toilets. Phrases such as "slaving over the stove" and the "drudgery of cooking" abounded in advertisements, along with "You Deserve a Break Today" and other slogans that reinforced the slaving, repetitive, and boring dimensions of cooking.

Unfortunately, the women's movement also encouraged the adoption of processed food. Women contributed significantly to the labor pool needed for the Allies' victory in WWII. They worked in munitions and food factories, operated machines, pumped gas, and delivered mail. With the return of soldiers, most of the women went back to homemaking—some quite happily and some with frustration and resentment. The emancipation of women in 1920 gave women the right to vote, and seeking equal educational and economic opportunities became the focus of the movement, although it went into a period of dormancy during WWI and WWII. The women's movement in the 1960s and 1970s is better known for fighting to broaden women's reproductive and sexual choices, but it also continued to fight for legislation that would prohibit discrimination in hiring and pay practices in the workplace. Out of a desire for meaningful careers and the sheer economic necessity of bringing money into the family, increasing numbers of women went to work.

According to a 2013 US Bureau of Labor Statistics report, 68 percent of married mothers and 75 percent of unmarried mothers leave their homes for paid work.[2] Although women now earn a significant portion of the household income, what hasn't much changed is the breakdown of household chores. Women still do most of the cooking, so working mothers put in a double shift, as it were. They work eight hours a day at a job and then come home to laundry, cleaning, overseeing homework, teachers' meetings, doctor's appointments, *and* cooking. Making nutritious meals for the family is often just another task added to a very full plate. As a result, convenience foods start looking, well, *convenient*, and food pretty much loses any symbolic association with the sacred, such as reminding us of God's grace-filled sustaining presence in the world. Cooking becomes a matter of getting sustenance into bodies to keep family members going and perhaps also the pleasure in coming home to food that only needs warming up.

Rethinking Drudgery

Most days I love to cook—at least nine out of ten. It is not drudgery. As a writer and part-time farmer, I have the fortune of structuring my days, so I can take time to cook. Calypso beans that I soaked last night (adding a splash of oil and a toss of salt) have already been cooked this morning and are ready to mix with sautéed onions, garlic, chopped sweet potatoes, dried cayenne pepper (just a tad), and homemade tomato sauce. Their flavors will marry as they slowly bake into a warm and hearty casserole for supper tonight.

Flexible structuring hasn't always described my days. The most challenging years were the three that I commuted an hour to teach at Trinity International University in Deerfield, Illinois. Mark attended the parent-teacher meetings and took care of anything that came up during the day. The forgotten lunch, for instance, or the *few* times the police department called about our dog, Chále, who had again jumped the fence in search of playmates. Mark reminds me of this occasionally (although he would say Chále jumped the fence *many* times) when he's looking to gain some traction in conversations about adding animals at Fern Creek.

During and after those years—because we had grown accustomed to it—everyone grabbed his or her own breakfast (cold cereal) except on Sunday, when we treated ourselves to Costco muffins. The first year I commuted, Mark packed a lunch for whoever wanted one, but in the years that followed, everyone fended for themselves. We kept on hand supplies from Costco that could be assembled easily—supplies that now make me shudder—like chips and granola bars and juice boxes. We managed dinner better. We grilled a lot of chicken breasts (Costco) to eat with rice, made breakfast for dinner about once a week, and ate out with whoever was free on Fridays. Any daughter willing to make dinner for the family earned five dollars; Megan Anna (a sixth grader when we started this practice) cooked nearly every week, while her sisters cooked a bit more sporadically. Mark became an efficient and good cook during those years—churning out chicken curry, tacos, chili, and pizza in thirty minutes.

As I recount that period in our lives, I realize that the upside of working an hour away was that everyone had ample opportunity to play in the kitchen if they wanted to. While we tried to avoid eating with convenience in mind, we weren't eating very intentionally, nor were we thinking about local, seasonal, or ethical food.

So while I had less openness in my days, cooking didn't feel like drudgery even then because we all shared the tasks of feeding the family. I loved cooking when I took the time and had the energy for it. Mark and I eat better now than we did when our daughters lived at home with us, and I wish we had known better then to be as intentional as we are now.

In more recent years, I've worked ten minutes from home and have looked forward to days when I got home early enough to give an entire hour over to the creation of our evening meal. On days when I couldn't, Mark and I cooked together, and I loved those times too. The tensions of the day fell away as we chopped and sautéed vegetables for a frittata or stir-fry or soup, talking about this and that, nurturing each other's body and soul.

In 2011, Bosch Appliances surveyed one thousand men and women about their cooking practices, asking what kept them out of the kitchen.[3] Setting aside qualms about why the survey was conducted (by a company that sells appliances to make cooking easier), the results are rather enlightening. Half of the people surveyed don't cook because their partner does all the cooking. (I find this more good news than bad, in that *someone* apparently is cooking.) Nearly a third don't cook because they don't know how to cook, which likely overlaps with the first reason. A quarter of those surveyed can't stand the mess, and two out of three find grocery shopping their most time-consuming household chore (I agree wholeheartedly on this point). Finally, one in five say they don't have time to cook. As I said, these results are better than I would have expected.

The Harris Poll also uncovered heartening news. In 2010 they asked over 2,500 people whether they love, enjoy, or dislike cooking. While 79 percent of people said they enjoy it (by answering either "I love it" or "I enjoy it when I have the time"), 30 percent said they love it. Only 14 percent said they do not enjoy cooking, and 7 percent said they don't cook.[4] On the whole, people report less drudgery than advertising leads us to believe.

Before I met with Michael and Brandon to talk about cooking, I assumed I knew what they would say. Both men stay home with their children and carry the primary responsibility for homemaking tasks while their wives leave home to work in the paid labor force. I expected Brandon and Michael to say that they enjoy cooking, but sure, drudgery is part of the story.

I was wrong. Over tea and coffee at Chapters, a local bookstore and coffee shop, I laid out my spiel about drudgery—its historic causes and the role of food corporations. They listened politely with what I would describe as blank expressions, which didn't seem like a great way to start the conversation. But as it turned out, they had a lot to say. Early on we decided that the notion of drudgery as it relates to cooking may be a gendered response, and the more I thought on it, the more it made sense. Neither Brandon nor Michael absorbed messages that suggested they needed to be saved from the kitchen because cooking was beneath their dignity (nor did I get the sense that they felt like cleaning a toilet was beneath them, though—to be clear—neither of them suggested cleaning toilets inspired any sense of creativity). We decided that maybe women who grew up being expected to take on the role of cook were primed to feel "condemned" to it. Michael and Brandon easily embraced cooking because it was a choice, nothing they felt compelled to do. It expressed their creativity in a way that also met the practical need of feeding their families. Michael said, "Cooking is a challenge, a creative process. It feeds part of me." Brandon echoed his sentiments.

That's not to say they hadn't internalized a cultural message that did more harm than good. The pressure they both felt was to be productive, to have something to show for their day's work. For them, cooking dinner became that end-of-the-line, tangible accomplishment. As it turns out, the cultural message they received reinforces cooking as a creative, legitimate, and good use of time and talent, unlike the kinds of messages women received that undermined a positive relationship with cooking.

I walked back to my car enthralled after our conversation. In part I was energized by our shared enthusiasm for carrots, lentils, cumin, and thyme, but more than that, I left hoping that maybe together women could reject messages that turn cooking into drudgery and see it instead as an earthy, need-fulfilling expression of creativity. What would it take to free women from that collective expectation to cook so that they could say, "I *choose* to cook—to exercise my creative capacity to transform gifts of creation into nourishing sustenance"?

A good bit of hope infuses the corporate food story as well. What is being called the Great Recession (also the Global Recession), which began in December 2007, wreaked a good deal of havoc around the globe. But the recession also sparked, as recessions and depressions in the last 150 years have consistently done, a turn toward home. Some people who were laid off found themselves with more time than money and started experimenting with raw, basic food ingredients. Even after the economy started rebounding, enough people had rubbed shoulders with others exploring good food options that they stayed with it. People tasted food they'd prepared themselves and were astonished, satisfied at having created something so tantalizingly good.

Food blogs continue to grow in number and popularity every year. Recipes get shared on Facebook, Pinterest, and Twitter. What began out of economic necessity has taken root and flourished. People from all social classes are seeing food industries less as a solution for busy families and more as a troubling contributor to high rates of diabetes, heart disease, and obesity.

When it came to social class and drudgery, I held a stereotype about the poor that embarrasses me now. I wrongly assumed that families in lower income brackets don't cook, and my thinking went something like this. The working poor do work that truly *is* drudgery. They scrub floors and clean toilets at fast-food restaurants; they clean toilets, tubs, and change beds in motels and hotels across America. They do laundry for nursing homes and hospitals, shine shoes, and collect garbage. They come home bone tired and not overly eager to stand in front of a stove to cook. Because they don't know *how* to cook—so my reasoning went—they also don't know much about nutrition, so they eat at McDonald's and consume ramen noodles and macaroni and cheese.

Yet a survey of 1,500 low- and middle-income families conducted by Share Our Strength, a nonprofit working to end hunger in the United States, challenges that stereotype. They discovered that the lower a family's income, the more they cooked from "scratch." Seventy-eight percent cooked or ate at home five or more nights a week and got take-out food or ate at a restaurant less than once a week. Of the meals cooked at home, four were dinners made from scratch, and two were partially supplemented or packaged meals. While 85 percent of respondents said that healthy eating was important to them, only half felt they achieved it. The biggest barriers are the predictable ones: the cost of wholesome foods and time.[5] Lower-income families are less limited by knowledge, it turns out, than by access to affordable food and time at home to cook it.

As this research shows, the crisis is not that no one is cooking or likes cooking; everyone is not eating at McDonald's or Pizza Hut five nights a week. Maybe a silver lining of the Great Recession looks something like the practice of rationing: most of us can't afford to go out as often as we used to, and when our alternative becomes SpaghettiOs versus pasta primavera made from scratch, we start experimenting.

The truth is that all work includes elements akin to drudgery, perhaps better described as *weariness*. Changing diapers, washing toilets, weeding vegetables, tending the young and old and sick, teaching, programming, selling, assembling, and cooking can all make one weary—even weary to the bone. Work, at least good work, is good because it promotes the flourishing of life. It spreads affection. Perhaps what is required to reclaim cooking (and other sometimes wearisome and laborious tasks of daily living) is to see them for what they can be: creative hand-, head-, and heartfelt expressions of love.

An Invitation to Good Work

Within every meal lies the hope of life sustained and the potential for creativity.

Any morning I enter the kitchen and add oats from the pantry to water on the stove I reflect something of God's sustaining nature. Toss in a spoonful of flax seed, a sprinkle of cinnamon, and a chopped apple or a handful of berries (fresh in the summer, frozen in the winter), and I have become a craftsman. Add affection for God, God's creation, and

❦ *Money in the United States* ❦
Who Has What Part of the Pie?

Hardly anyone blames the working poor for their poverty. And yet in the United States we tolerate gross inequality as though *not* to tolerate it challenges freedoms defined by the American dream. Maybe people don't know how severe the inequality is.

Allow me to get specific. The top 1 percent of Americans have 40 percent of all the wealth in the United States, while the bottom 80 percent (yes, *80*) have 7 percent of the wealth. The poorest 20 percent have access to the smallest portion of that wealth. They are underemployed, earn minimum wage, struggle from paycheck to paycheck, and barely get by. The other 60 percent belong to a hard-working middle class that doesn't look a whole lot healthier than the working poor beneath them. Seven percent of the wealth in the United States doesn't spread far among 80 percent of a population.

Minimum wage gives these numbers some context. In 2014, the Federal Minimum Wage (some states offer higher or lower minimum

Mark—who will eat with me—and according to Francis of Assisi, I am an artist. Cooking is good work.

Christians believe we carry God's image within us, which is historically understood in functional and relational ways. We function as thinking, feeling, acting members of creation—standing in for God, as it were—to be the stewards who care for creation. We also reflect something of God's image as we relate to each other, work, play, and even cook. Reflecting God's image in the kitchen requires us to stop thinking about food only as body-fuel and see it as one of God's primary ways to express divine provision. And we can't make the trade without a reverence for creation. Getting there, as theologian Norman Wirzba says, "entails spiritual formation in which we allow God the Gardener (Gen. 2:8) to conform us to his image as the one who looks after and provides for creatures."[6] If food is one of God's most abiding and daily love languages, then preparing food puts us smack dab in the center of a deeply spiritual and physical process that

wages) was set at $7.25/hour, which comes to $14,500/year for a full-time worker paid for fifty weeks/year. That comes to $1,200 a month. Assuming rent is a modest $400 and all food expenses total a modest $500, that doesn't leave much money for clothes, utilities, doctor's appointments, a cell phone, or eating at McDonald's. Even if a household of four has two full-time workers, $2,400/month doesn't go very far, especially if child care is an additional expense. In 2012, 59 percent of all hourly workers were paid minimum wage, but half of those were under the age of twenty-five; it's understandable that a sixteen-year-old would get paid significantly less to flip a burger than, say, a thirty-six-year-old. This means that nearly 30 percent of all adult (over the age of twenty-five) hourly wage workers receive a salary that doesn't keep them above the poverty line set by the government each year. In 2012, that line was $23,000 for a family of four. Two adults working full-time barely exceed that number.

Still, most of the working poor want to feed their families better. They cook more than not and certainly know more than I've given them credit for knowing. They do what they can with what they have.

begins and ends in the arms of God. Once we see food as God's loving, tangible provision, we find it in the snap peas in the freezer, the onions in the cellar, and the barley in the pantry. Working with tangible expressions of God's love becomes holy work, good work.

Cooking is sacramental when we recognize that feeding ourselves and others is what enables our embodied souls to make and tend children; care for aging parents, friends, and strangers; plant and harvest; speak words of grace, gratitude, and forgiveness; fight for justice; and extend mercy. Any good accomplished happens because someone went into a kitchen to prepare food. We reflect God's love for the cosmos even more fully when that food is also good for God's sustaining earth and our neighbors next door and around the world.

Definitions of good work throughout the centuries don't vary greatly. Three characteristics emerge. First, good work is meaningful, that is, *it makes the world a better place*. Second, good work is done with a *commitment to excellence*, which can be the characteristic we find easiest to focus on. Third, good work is ethical, in that *it contributes to flourishing* for the one doing the work, those for whom the work is done, and for whatever parts of creation (animals, farmland, forests, atmosphere, water sources) that are used to complete it.

Wendell Berry expresses this all-encompassing view with a definition that applies to all forms of work, including cooking. Berry says that the name of our proper connection to the earth is "good work," for good work involves much giving of honor. It honors the source of its materials; it honors the place where it is done; it honors the art by which it is done; it honors the thing that it makes and the user of the made thing.[7]

Cooking is not much honored in our culture. Imagine how different cooking might feel if our collective habit was to honor cooks, whole foods, kitchen spaces, the craft of cooking, the prepared food itself, and the people who eat it.

Redeeming the word *homemaker* could be a starting place. I asked Michael and Brandon how they felt about the term "stay-at-home dad." I wondered whether the term captured for them their role as chef, tender of children, and manager of other work required to keep a home. Michael said:

> I don't really know how to refer to my occupation. *Stay-at-home dad* is off-putting for the same reasons that *stay-at-home mom* is off-putting to many

women. *Homemaker* is the closest recognizable term I've heard; of course, that brings up images of plump, doting wives rearranging dried flower arrangements, so it's not perfect. I don't think our culture values parents enough who personally raise their children to come up with a name that truly captures that role.[8]

Brandon, Michael, and all sorts of mostly invisible women and men are doing good work in their homes. They nurture the human spirit and body using hands, head, and heart. They help life to flourish—not only their own and their family's but also the lives of their communities. Some of them foster all kinds of life above and beneath the soil as they tend gardens and grow food.

Somewhere along the way we determined that good work involved getting paid, and the more we got paid, the better the work. Meaning, excellence, and ethics came to be defined by concepts like growth, competition, and efficiency. But what if the *best* work reflects who God is as the creator and sustainer of life? God supplied a sacrificial ram for Abraham, manna and water for the Israelites during their sojourn in the wilderness, and ravens with food for Elijah while he hid from Ahab and Jezebel. God even feeds the ravens when their young cry out (Job 38:41). The God portrayed in the Old Testament is very earthy, attending to material matters like food.

Perhaps it shouldn't be so difficult to imagine God hoeing onions or checking on beehives or fishing or baking bread. Jesus, in whom we see God, gathered children into his lap, fed the hungry, healed the sick, wept on behalf of Jerusalem, and, at least once, made breakfast for his disciples.

As poet Mary Oliver writes in her poem, "Messenger":

> My work is loving the world. . . .
> which is mostly standing still and learning to be
>   astonished. . . .
> which is gratitude, to be given a mind and a heart
>   and these body-clothes,
> a mouth with which to give shouts of joy.[9]

May we stretch toward living so that every movement reflects God's Light within, God's sustaining love that holds the world. May our work be good, even—especially—in the kitchen.

⤙ Six Gadgetless, Simple, ⤚ Sometimes Essential Cooking Tools

Good work often requires tools. Here's a starter kit for the kitchen. Some complaints about cooking come from a lack of confidence more than anything. However much one might want to engage cooking as good work with sacramental love, if one lacks confidence, cooking with any measure of joy is difficult. So whether you take or leave these "tools," they are intended to boost confidence and start home fires burning.

1. The Well-Stocked Pantry

With some measure of confidence I offer you a composite of four basic lists for a well-stocked pantry: Mark's, Michael's, Brandon's, and mine. They are satisfyingly similar.

Baking and Cooking

- Whole wheat and white flour (gluten-free flours as necessary)
- Baking powder, baking soda, kosher or sea salt, yeast
- Oils (olive, canola)
- Sweeteners (brown and white sugar, also honey, maple syrup, molasses, or agave, according to preference)
- Dried herbs (oregano, thyme, rosemary) and spices (cinnamon, paprika, cumin, curry)
- Vinegars (apple cider, red wine, balsamic), lemon juice, soy sauce
- Dried fruit (at least raisins)
- Seeds and nuts (store large quantities in the freezer)
- Baking cocoa

Items for Simple Meals

- Dried beans, lentils, split peas, grains (e.g., wheat berries, oatmeal, brown rice, quinoa)

- Canned tomatoes, canned beans, canned pumpkin (one can do *so much* with frozen, canned, or fresh winter squash)
- Vegetable and/or chicken stock (frozen, canned, or store-bought)
- Dry pasta/noodles

Basic Dairy and Refrigerated Proteins

- Eggs (from a local source, if possible, and/or from chickens raised outside eating grass and bugs, which increases omega-3 fatty acids and the happiness of the chickens)
- Butter (similarly, the healthiest and best-for-you, best-for-the-cow butter is from pasture-based cows) or butter equivalent (Earth Balance is a healthy vegan choice)
- Cheeses (an assortment of hard, semisoft, soft, and crumbled varieties, such as parmesan, cheddar, goat, feta)
- Milk (preferably without the growth hormone rBGH) or milk substitute
- Peanut butter and/or almond butter

In the Produce Drawer and Refrigerator

- Onions, garlic, sweet and regular potatoes in a drawer/basket not in the refrigerator (where they sprout and soften)
- Carrots, celery, and other seasonal vegetables and greens
- Seasonal fruit (if it's not in season, don't buy it)
- A mustard or two and pickled something or other (capers, dilly beans, and/or pickles to lift limp salads and invigorate sandwiches, sauces, or oneself)

In the Freezer

- Frozen peas, corn, cooked winter squash, berries
- Frozen meats (local, pasture-based, humanely raised)
- Bread (a back-up loaf)

With a well-stocked pantry and a bit of courageous experimenting, anyone can whip up a dinner in thirty minutes or less.

2. Simple Meal Planning

Lots of thoughtful people have provided systems for meal planning. Here's what works for me when I'm disciplined enough to do it, which is only sometimes. Since I keep a well-stocked pantry, planning is not critical. Still, before I make a trip to the grocery store I figure out a flexible menu for the week. If I get stuck in the figuring, I have a few strategies:

1. Ask Mark what he'd like for dinner in the next week. He feels (unnecessarily) guilty for not helping as much in the kitchen now that I can structure my day as I please. I capitalize on this guilt by asking what he wants for dinner. He knows I'm asking because I am stuck, so he always comes through. Even when I don't like his ideas, asking him gets me unstuck. Sometimes it's because I realize I like the ideas I have not yet thought of better than the ones he has given me. This is not fair to him, but it's how it is; and he accepts it graciously.
2. Pull out a cookbook for inspiration. Just this week I tried three new recipes from *Nourishing Meals: Healthy Gluten-Free Recipes for the Whole Family*, by Alissa Segersten and Tom Malterre. This is an excellent resource even if you eat gluten, which we do. The Calypso bean and sweet potato dish I described earlier—except for a few substitutions and tweaks—came from *Nourishing Meals*.
3. Ask one of my daughters what she's cooking for dinner. Megan Anna is the one who recommended *Nourishing Meals* to me. Sarah has a vegan cooking blog. Generally whatever they are cooking, I want.
4. When I'm really stuck I go through my standard repertoire and choose one breakfast dinner meal (frittata usually, sometimes waffles), one soup (or main dish salad in the summer), one meal that uses tofu, one that highlights beans or lentils, one that uses

some form of fish or meat, and one that highlights a grain or pasta. The meals always include lots of vegetables, which in the winter come from the freezer, pantry, or root cellar. Since I make meals from leftover bits and pieces, the menu-planning list doesn't play out very precisely. Which is fine by me. Any plan I come up with is flexible. But a plan helps get me unstuck.

3. Create an Honorable Kitchen Space

Wendell Berry talks about good work honoring the place where work is done. On some level that simply means keeping dishes out of the sink and stray oil, mustard, and honey wiped off the countertops. For me it also means not filling the counters with appliances like mixers and blenders and toasters. I keep them stashed away but close at hand. Donell, one of my dear friends, gave me a metal rooster that her friend made. Mr. Rooster sits on the counter behind my sink and greets me several times a day. I am reminded of cooking adventures with Donell and her enduring friendship when I see it. Windows above the sink look out over Fern Creek toward the big woods and bring something of life that is outside inside, reminding me where my food originates. No matter how small or impractical or unsatisfying, find a way to bring lightheartedness, warmth, and expressions of gratitude into the kitchen to create an inviting, honorable space.

4. Five Things You Don't Need to Buy Prepackaged

Some things are easy to make and taste way better than the processed alternatives at the grocery store (such as rye and graham crackers). Some are hard to make but still taste better than the processed alternatives (marshmallows), and some are not particularly hard to make but are more time consuming and still worth it on occasion (vegetable stock). Below are five examples of super easy things to make that taste way better than what one can get prepackaged or processed.

1. *Popcorn.* How is it, that in one generation we have stopped popping popcorn on the stove in a pan? All one needs is pop-

corn, salt, oil, and a pan with a lid (the lid is important). Both the salt and oil amounts can be adjusted to taste. Heat 1½ tablespoons of oil in a pan on medium-high heat. Add 2 or 3 kernels and cover. When one of them pops, add ½ cup popcorn and a teaspoon of salt. Keep the pan moving (shake, jiggle) until the popping has just about stopped so that the popcorn doesn't burn. Remove from heat, pour into a bowl, and enjoy. Adding additional butter is optional. We now have a stovetop popcorn maker, which works better with our glass-top range. These come with a hand crank that we turn during the popping to keep the popcorn moving, replacing the pot shaking/jiggling.

2. *Salad dressing.* The best salad dressing is freshly made. If I'm adding garlic and want it especially creamy I use a little food processor my mother-in-law gave me twenty-five years ago; otherwise I put the ingredients in a pint jar with a lid and give it a good shake. Assuming that several oils, vinegars, spices, and garlic are in the pantry, great salad dressing can be whisked together in less than three minutes. Start with this ratio: one part vinegar to one-and-a-half parts oil. Adapt depending on how light or heavy or how much bite (more vinegar) or smoothness (more oil) is desired. Add salt and pepper and some herbs. Play. Make a honey mustard by combining a good bit of Dijon or yellow mustard with a little bit of honey (optional), lemon juice, and olive oil. Experiment with bits, dollops, and pinches instead of teaspoons and tablespoons and discover that there are fewer rules governing cooking than one might imagine. Make balsamic vinegar dressing with balsamic vinegar, olive oil, crushed garlic, oregano, thyme, salt, and pepper. I like making this one in the food processor because it blends and thickens, and I can bypass crushing the garlic. Taste it, and if it's too acidic, add a pinch of sugar, a bit of honey, or more oil. Use orange juice, lemon juice, and olive oil with a bit of mint, salt, and pepper for a delightfully fresh spring dressing. Taste, taste, taste (dipping with a piece of

spinach or cucumber) and adjust accordingly. Specific directions for salad dressings abound on the internet if my vagueness is troubling.

3. *Muffins and pancake mixes.* A well-stocked pantry will have all one needs to make muffins, cakes, pancakes, and brownies. A mix only shortens the process by two minutes, maybe three. I am not kidding. A mix has precombined the dry ingredients, often including powdered milk, powdered egg, and a bunch of non-food extras that sound frightful when you read the label. Mark and I disagree about one particular boxed mix. I cannot convince him that my brownies taste better than brownies from a box. It might be because his taste has been shaped (distorted) from years of eating brownies from a box. It might be because the particular boxed brownies he likes are triple chocolate and probably triple fat and sugar as well. Still, when we made them side by side (we did this in the name of taste testing), he finished no more than two minutes before me. Mixes don't save time, but they make these foods possible for people who don't have well-stocked pantries.

4. *Refrigerator biscuits and cookies.* While I'm on the subject of mixes, let me say three words about refrigerator/biscuit rolls that come in a tube that pops open when you twist it or knock it on the counter and cookie dough that comes in a plastic-wrapped cylinder: just say no. They save a very small amount of time (*maybe* five minutes) and are intended for people who do not have a well-stocked pantry. But the convenience comes at such cost in flavor! A side-by-side taste test shows that there is no comparison. But again, I can imagine one's taste being shaped (distorted) from years of eating this stuff. Mark can put together a batch of chocolate chip cookies *and* a batch of his amazing biscuits (I do *not* recommend making both of these with the intention of eating them in the same night) in the time it takes me to put together minestrone soup, which requires a fair amount of chopping. And speaking of soup . . .

5. *Canned soup.* First off, I admit that I keep a couple cans of Amy's Soups in my pantry. They might be more than a year old, but sometimes, especially when I'm sick and don't feel up to making chicken noodle soup (my absolute favorite when I have a cold), then a can of Amy's lentil soup serves me well enough. But if I have vegetable or turkey stock in my pantry (made from the Thanksgiving turkey) and some kind of grain or legume (split peas, lentils, barley, brown rice), an onion, a couple of carrots, and some celery, all the basics for a great soup are at my fingertips. Even without all those ingredients, one can make a great soup out of a stocked pantry, freezer, and root cellar. For variety, add heat, like a dried cayenne pepper with as many of the seeds as you dare and/or tomato sauce and/or a splash of red wine or vinegar and/or other vegetables (corn, potatoes, kale, spinach, cabbage), some herbs, maybe small pasta noodles, salt, and pepper. Or sauté an onion, add a chopped apple and some peeled and chopped winter squash (or thaw some from the freezer or use a can of pumpkin), good vegetable broth, a bit of salt, pepper, and cumin. Cook until the squash is tender (or warmed through if using frozen or canned), and then puree with an immersion blender or in a full-sized blender. This will be delicious as is, or make it more velvety by stirring in ⅓–½ cup of half-and-half right before serving, if some happens to be sitting in the fridge. Wonderful butternut squash soup can be created in less than thirty minutes. It's better than any soup that comes from a can.

For cooking to become a creative outlet, it is important to play with ingredients and worry less about following a recipe. I use recipes when I need inspiration or am trying to make a brownie Mark will prefer to his triple chocolate box, but more of my cooking involves figuring out what I have on hand, what sounds good, and experimenting.

5. Change Your Relationship with Recipes

Making soups was my starting point for deviating from recipes. Recipes are useful when confidence needs boosting and one hasn't yet figured out how certain ingredients play together in the kettle. My first deviations were simply the product of finding substitutes for ingredients I didn't have. While I make all kinds of substitutions in various cookie, quick bread, and yeast bread recipes, I attend to dry-to-wet ratios when baking. Thinking about recipes as guides rather than rules is freeing. Thinking creatively about how to turn leftovers from one meal into some piece of the next one becomes an engaging challenge. The creative cook might roast a whole pan of vegetables and then use them in various ways throughout the week—maybe as a side dish, then in a sandwich or egg frittata, next as the vegetables in a noodle or rice dinner, then on pizza or a galette, and finally, tossed into a soup. A book that inspires creativity and gives a good bit of culinary guidance is *An Everlasting Meal* by Tamar Adler.

6. Create Cooking Opportunities with Others

Anyone with a kitchen large enough to accommodate two people can invite at least one other person to cook with them. Cooking with someone else adds interest, perspective, and companionship. During the CSA season, once a week the farmers (Mark and me) and apprentices (two or three others) cook and eat dinner together. One particularly adventurous year we decided to cook dinner by pairing up in every possible combination. The cooking pair planned the menu, decided where we'd eat (we ate up in the tree house, down in the gazebo, in the courtyard, and at the picnic table), laid the table, cooked the food, and cleaned up afterward. Those of us not cooking that night felt tenderly cared for. It was a sacramental meal for us all.

When our children were at home we sometimes set aside regular times for them to cook with one of us, though the most magical times happened more spontaneously. A picture of Mark and Rae in aprons, making donuts together (deep fried, sugary, terrible-for-you donuts) makes me smile still.

Some people establish or join cooking clubs, where participants come together and cook meals that can be frozen for the month ahead (or some variant thereof). Some working couples set aside time on weekends, doing the good work of creating meals together for the week ahead.

I bake with my grandchildren but not enough to satisfy them. Auden asks me periodically when I'll bake with her again. That she asks warms my heart and keeps me mindful of this opportunity I have to shape her relationship with pots and pans and flour and noodles and beans and spinach.

Communion at the table is richer when we work together to provide each other's sustenance. Joining friends, children, and spouses in the kitchen to bake cookies or knead bread or cook dinner together at the end of the day is to begin communion in the kitchen—tangible and good work transforming God's creation into pleasurable sustenance.

• *Roasted Summer Vegetable Pizza with Pesto Tomato Sauce* • *(Makes 1 Medium Pizza)*

If not using a premade crust, make the pizza dough first. A basic recipe is below. Otherwise, preheat oven to 350 degrees.

1. Heat 1–2 teaspoons olive oil in skillet. Slice a sweet onion (e.g., Walla Walla) and caramelize it by cooking on medium to low heat while the other vegetables roast in the oven.
2. Slice 5–6 medium-sized tomatoes, a summer squash, and ½–1 cup broccoli florets (substitute other vegetables as desired but keep the onions and tomatoes constant). Drizzle with olive oil, season with salt, and roast in preheated 350-degree oven for about 25 minutes, stirring occasionally.
3. Meanwhile, prepare the sauce. Stir 3 tablespoons pesto with 3 tablespoons tomato paste (freeze the rest of the paste in ice cube trays and store in the freezer for later). Thin to a spreadable consistency with about 1 tablespoon of tomato juice, stock, or water. (Freeze and store juice off drained tomatoes in ice cube trays for times such as this.) As an alternative, use a jar of pizza sauce and add some pesto, or omit the pesto altogether. Remember, recipes are guidelines.
4. Spread sauce on crust or prepared dough, top with roasted vegetables, then add thinly sliced basil and hot pepper flakes (optional). Crumble a bit of feta cheese or place thinly sliced fresh mozzarella over the top. Bake according to the directions for whatever crust you are using. Cool 5–10 minutes. Slice and enjoy.

Pizza Dough Recipe

1. Soften 1 scant tablespoon yeast (or 1 package) in ¾ cup warm water (about 5 minutes or until the yeast starts to bubble).
2. Stir in 1 teaspoon sugar, 2 tablespoons oil, and 1 teaspoon salt. Add 1½ cups flour and stir until well blended. Work in another ½ cup or so. The dough should not stick to your hands.
3. Transfer to an oiled bowl, cover with a towel, and set in a warm place until it doubles in size, about an hour. Roast the rest of the vegetables (see recipe above); once they are out of the oven, increase the temperature to 400 degrees.
4. Turn dough onto a floured counter or breadboard and knead a few times. Let rest 10 minutes. Stretch and toss and pull gently to create a thin, circular crust. Place on an oiled and cornmeal-sprinkled pizza pan or baking sheet and continue to flatten and stretch into a circle. Lightly brush with olive oil, add toppings as described above, and bake for about 15 minutes—until the crust is golden. Cool 5 minutes before eating.

Reflections and Questions

1. List the first three food-related or restaurant slogans that come to mind. Since they are rumbling around in your head, how might each one have shaped your thoughts or choices about cooking or eating in the last week or month?
2. Does reading this history of food processing, world war rations, and expanding roles for women help explain any part of your own relationship to cooking over the years? If so, how?
3. Good work is discussed throughout the book and defined in this chapter. Reflect on the kinds of work you currently do. In what ways does your work fulfill or fall short of the definition provided in this chapter?
4. For many women the term *homemaker* has become somewhat complicated and conflicted. Are we—both men and women—to embrace or resist homemaking as a chosen path? Does it mean we are selling out if we do not stay home and "home make" or failing to live up to our potential if we do? In what ways do Brandon's and Michael's experience with homemaking, and specifically their positive feelings

about cooking for their families, surprise you? What does their experience add to the conversation?

5. The chapter cites research about low-income families and their cooking/eating patterns. Does any of it challenge your perceptions of low-income families or thoughts about public policy? Does it raise any additional questions or thoughts worth pondering or discussing?

6. Maybe God yearns to be with us in our kitchens as much as Auden yearns to share Lisa's. What would it look like to welcome God into your kitchen?

3
Preservation

The choice for your way has to be made every moment of my life. I have to choose thoughts that are your thoughts, words that are your words, and actions that are your actions. There are no times or places without choices. And I know how deeply I resist choosing you.

—Henri Nouwen, a Lenten prayer[1]

One warm, golden-hued October day last fall, I took a friend kayaking on the Willamette River. We'd been talking about Wendell Berry, which meant we spent more than a little time discussing growing and eating food and the fragile yet resilient nature of community. On that morning our conversation meandered, as rivers and conversations are wont to do, into an estuary where life intersects faith.

She had moved on from the faith of her youth. She might say she "outgrew it," or something of that sort. We trust each other well enough that I dared to ask what she thought of my faith, to which I have clung tenaciously but also have done battle with. Honestly, I wondered what she thought of me. I might have asked if she thought me "naive," but I don't remember. I'd like to think I left the question dangling, neither putting words into her mouth nor making her feel like she had to say something nice, faith-affirming, or Lisa-affirming.

After a few quiet paddle strokes she said, "*Fidelity*. That's the word that comes to mind. You have been faithful to your faith." We both paddled some more, and then she said, "I think your faith is beautiful, and part of me wishes I had the grounding your faith gives you. My spiritual self roams, and while I prefer it that way, sometimes I miss something more rooted."

We said more about this then (and since), but it's the word *fidelity* that has stuck with me. It is a good word—one that describes commitment that may waver, though never very far, and a willingness to limit certain choices in order to fulfill the obligations of fidelity. Fidelity preserves relationships and ways of living in the world, one choice at a time. Choices, strung together like so many twinkling lights, mark the way and become habits of the heart. Sometimes choice and habit become a fidelity so strong that infidelity becomes unthinkable. But often enough, preserving a thing we care about requires paying attention to choices that keep the habits strong.

We preserve and become faithful to all sorts of things—faith, hobbies, marriage, exercise, eating habits, compassion, generosity. Many of our choices make the world a hope-filled and flourishing place. Some habits (addictions come to mind) destroy us and those around us.

So yes, as humans we preserve a lot more than food. My mother gave me a quilt that my grandma made for Mom and Dad as a wedding gift, hand stitching into each teal, cream, and white triangle her hopes and dreams for them, her support and enduring love. Mom used it only occasionally, and now it covers our guest bed, a beautiful symbol of love and marriage several generations old.

We pass down values about how to treat children, spouses, parents, and siblings. We pass down our ways of life and sense of obligation to neighbors, to the land we live on, and to future generations. We pass down canning jars and relish recipes. Some of this gets picked up and some laid down, but fidelity is about what *we* do—our faithfulness—rather than what future generations do with what we pass on.

God's grace-filled presence throughout the universe means that every generation experiences anew God's love and purposes for creation and has the chance to preserve and pass on both the seen and unseen. Could opening a jar of home-canned green beans remind us of, and make us grateful for, the fidelity of those who figured things out and passed down values and skills, making the life we're living possible?

In my best moments, my most attentive moments, I'm inspired to remember that I belong not to myself but to God, to the history and future of humanity, and to the creation out of which I draw life. I want to preserve what God loves. While I'm limited a fair bit in my efforts, I can still be faithful and love my precious speck in the universe. Out of a jar of homemade tomato sauce can spill gratitude and the choice to be faithful.

As much as I love preserving food, I'm not audacious enough to think it a Christian duty. Still, it gives me opportunity each season of the year to reflect on Christian values that help me find direction in life. Preserving food to slow down its natural decomposition is a simple and regular reminder that some things in life require a bit of forethought, intentional care, and attention to maintain their life-giving qualities.

About Nancy

Nancy, one of our enthusiastic community supported agriculture (CSA) members, preserves whatever she can get her hands on. She calls herself a bottom-feeder because she takes home "Grade B" produce (bruised apples, oversized zucchini, oddly shaped cucumbers)—extras that we set out for the taking that still taste good and look acceptable.

Nancy has spent twenty-five years as a psychologist and college professor, and she loves many things, including small-scale sustainable agriculture. However, she has a bit of a confidence gap in cooking and food preservation. She would say so herself. Nancy is always eager to learn new skills, and the last few years she's delved into local, seasonal food. She's attended a number of the Fern Creek Community Cooking Classes and planted a small, carefully researched heirloom fruit orchard; last year she added food preservation to her repertoire of skills. She canned applesauce, apple butter, and different kinds of pickles, and she froze green beans, corn, salsa, tomato puree, and berries. She stored potatoes, winter squash, onions, and garlic in her garage—a result of signing up for one of our Preservation Shares,[2] where she learned how to set food aside during the bounteous months for her family to eat throughout the winter.

Nancy crossed that confidence chasm and learned quite a bit about preserving over the course of five months. But at the beginning, Nancy approached the abundance with some apprehension, and most of her extra produce went into smoothies she fed her family.

Offering Preservation Shares helps us deal with extravagant bounty that goes beyond what we and our apprentices eat and preserve. Even so, last year we gifted the local food bank with buckets of beans, squash, and cucumbers.

We might be smart enough to figure out how much to grow so as to avoid such excess, but Mark overplants anyway. It helps him manage anxiety, but it also lets him be generous. I love that about him. Still, most years I give him grief for buying more onion seed, deciding we need yet another tray of broccoli seedlings, or thinking we should plant *something* in every empty space. I think about the work all that excess demands, but I try to move past that, wanting to be moved instead by a spirit of generosity. But I digress.

Preservation shareholders get extra berries, beans, broccoli, tomatoes, pickling cucumbers, apples, cabbage, and whatever else overproduces. They also receive dried beans, with names that match their beauty and unique flavors—Black Turtle, Calypso, Jacob's Cattle, Rattlesnake. In an evening class for those who want more confidence in food-preserving techniques, we wash, trim, slice, pressure can, ferment, pickle, and dehydrate an assortment of foods.

I've been asked what motivates me to preserve food by people who think it time-consuming and a dangerous hobby besides. I tell them I am drawn to danger and that this seems less dramatic than hopping freight trains, which I've also done (but only once, which was enough). But then I assure them that I am joking about the preserving. Let me say here: preserving food is no more dangerous than working with raw chicken. One just has to follow a few safety rules. In fact, it's less dangerous than getting in a car and driving to the grocery store; no matter how careful you are, you can still be blindsided by a careless driver.

The most obvious reason I preserve food is so that we can eat from our garden year-round. Preserving food is also economical. I don't mean that in the most obvious way; if you don't have to buy canned beans then of course you are saving money. But even if one has to buy local produce to preserve it, preserving food is economical when environmental costs are taken into account. The transportation of food from farms to processing plants and then to grocery stores has environmental costs. By doing so, our home (the earth), our atmosphere, and all living things bear the cost. Carbon is released into the air with the fuel burned to transport food hither and yon, and there's a lot of traveling hither and yon in the food industry. Add to that the trips taken to the grocery store to purchase it, and both personal and environmental costs go up.

I also preserve because it spurs creativity. I used to only put up the basics: green beans, applesauce, tomatoes, dill pickles. But then I started experimenting and haven't stopped since. Ketchup, corn salsa, pesto, sauerkraut, pickled beets, dilly beans, and smoked sweet peppers join the more standard fare in our pantry. Dressing up simple meals becomes easy when summer's flavors are captured in marvelous ways through creative food preservation.

Preserving food protects a history that belonged to our foreparents, whose planning ahead for winter was less optional or trendy; it was essential to eating well. Still, for our generation as well as theirs, lining jars of food on pantry shelves is deeply satisfying.

Come November, I stand in front of that pantry and feel hunkered in for winter. Quarts of dried beans, fruit, and grains; pints and quarts of canned goods; and a few quarts of Fern Creek honey grace the space. Bring on the winter storms! At best we will have one snow day per winter in Oregon (usually schools will simply open two hours late), but we're prepared for anything. Being ready for storms and the satisfaction of a full pantry must have felt different to generations that didn't have Thriftway or Kroger as an option when they ran out of beans or potatoes or applesauce.

Humans have always preserved what helped them survive: food, seeds, skills, knowledge, stories, and clan values and beliefs. When I heave the gallon jar I use for making sauerkraut off the pantry shelf, a whole history trails behind, following me into the kitchen. I don't have to figure out how to live well all by myself, how to store the abundance of summer and fall to feed my family. Generations of people before me figured it out bit by bit, leading the way toward plentiful, creative, and grateful eating year-round.

Nancy may call herself a bottom-feeder, perhaps feeling a bit sheepish about scooping up so much Grade B produce, but the word that comes to my mind is the same one my friend used on that kayaking trip—*fidelity*. Nancy invests in preserving healthy food for her family. She carries on a long human tradition of planning ahead, gratefully noticing the things that are worth preserving and valuing them enough to do the necessary work.

A History of Food Preservation

Environmental disasters, wars, and economic downturns remind us that plentiful food is not always available. The recent Great Recession showed the current generation that while we may be surrounded by food, our access to it can feel tentative. To make food supplies more secure, people are not just planting gardens in their backyards but putting back into practice ways of preserving food that have been in use for thousands of years.

Dehydration/Drying

Sun, beans—check. So easy. Which explains why drying foods has such a long history. Perhaps the first dried beans were happened upon; perhaps they were simply bean pods on bushes that had not been eaten by animals or people when they were fresh. Maybe these dry beans were gathered, brought home, ground into flour, or soaked in water and cooked to tenderness. Beans, corn, peas, and wheat could be left to dry in the field. They were then harvested and removed from the cob (corn) or pod (beans or peas) or stalk (grain) and kept for several years, during which time they were ground into flour for making cakes and breads, soaked and cooked into porridges and stews, or saved and planted in a subsequent year.

Perhaps dried fruits were discovered in the same way. Because drying fruits intensifies the sweetness of raisins, dates, prunes, figs, apricots, peaches, and apples, it offers a remnant of summer's sweet kiss long after the fruit-growing season ends. Dried herbs and spices can be added to dishes year-round and were used in trade, since dried spices and fruits are light and travel well over long distances.

Root Cellaring

Our ancestors stored carrots, potatoes, parsnips, cabbages, onions, beets, winter squash, apples, and pears in root cellars or caves, providing them with fall's harvest throughout the winter and early spring. The cooler temperatures slowed down spoilage, which would have occurred faster inside fire-warmed tents, teepees, and log cabins or, if left outside in fields, would freeze or be eaten by hungry field mice and rabbits. Today, people without a handy cave or root cellar store fall vegetables in basements, garages, and unheated bedrooms, or in plastic tubs placed into holes dug into the ground next to their homes.[3]

Fermentation

Food historians presume that fermentation was discovered rather than invented. Perhaps the first beer emerged from grains left in the rain, which fermented into something nasty smelling that one boy dared another boy to drink. Maybe fermented grapes came first. Regardless, once people left off their nomadic lives and settled down, they started growing all sorts of crops. Even Noah found vineyard-keeping and wine-making a pleasant pastime and an advantage to settling down.

Fermentation transforms cabbage into sauerkraut and kimchi; milk into yogurt and hard, soft, and semisoft cheeses; soybeans into tempeh and miso paste (a wonderful addition to vegetable soups and stocks); and black tea into kombucha. One downside of most ways of preserving food is that it removes nutrients, but fermenting adds them. Fermentation encourages microorganisms to work enzyme and probiotic magic that improves digestion, restoring the balance of bacteria in the gut.

Some forms of fermentation are an art form, and they've gained considerable popularity in the Willamette Valley where I live. Microbreweries, small wineries and creameries, and garage hobbyists are resurrecting small vineyards and cottage industries, deriving pleasure in honing wine-, beer-, and cheese-making skills.

Other forms of fermentation, like sauerkraut, require less skill but still involve a kind of magical transformation. One only needs cabbage, salt, a glass jar or crock, a waterproof plastic bag or a plate, and a rock. One also needs patience, which is not insignificant given how we've become used to the instant gratification of desire. One might also need a bit of courage to recognize the mold that grows on top of the jar as a bloom—a flower of sorts that signals fermentation is taking place.

Canning

Canning has a shorter history, which is related to feeding soldiers at war. During the wars between France and Great Britain at the opening of the nineteenth century, the French government offered a reward to anyone who came up with an efficient, effective way to preserve food that could travel with soldiers. The winner was a French confectioner and brewer who noticed that food sealed in glass jars didn't spoil as fast as foods left unsealed. However, glass jars were impractical for all sorts of reasons, so by 1810 the first canned tins emerged.

Canning is a simple process. Washed, fresh vegetables or fruits are put into a clean jar and filled with liquid (usually water). A lid with a rubber seal is screwed on top and then jars are submerged in a kettle of simmering water and boiled for a certain amount of time, depending on the food. This stops enzyme action, kills microorganisms, and seals the jar.

Although people didn't understand that bacteria was the culprit causing food to spoil until nearly fifty years after the French confectioner started canning foods, people could and did observe that canning and sealing food kept it from spoiling.

Freezing

Freezing food is both the oldest (along with drying) and newest process on the preservation scene. The first icehouse seems to have been built in 1780 BC in a Mesopotamian town. Winter snow, packed and insulated in icehouses, kept foods cool until the next winter's snowfall. Icehouses gave way to iceboxes, which made it possible for anyone able to pay for ice delivery to have refrigeration in their homes. Once humanity harnessed the power of electricity, other food preservation techniques slowly replaced older ones. Refrigerators showed up in the 1800s, and the ice delivery system didn't completely disappear in the United States until as late as the 1960s.

Once people had refrigerators and freezers in their homes, freezing food became practical for anyone with a backyard garden and space to spare in the freezer. Clarence Birdseye invented the technique that gave frozen foods a home in the grocery stores. In 1923 all Clarence wanted was year-round, fresh-tasting food for his family. After observing how people in the Arctic quick-froze their food, he came up with what became the commercial standard of quick-freezing to maximize and preserve the freshness, flavor, and nutritional value. Six years later, he sold his patents and trademarks for $22 million to an industry that was sure modern people would appreciate the freshness of frozen foods. And they did. Most people who freeze their own produce can't flash-freeze under high pressure like General Mills, but a quick blanching/cooling process allows peas, beans, broccoli, spinach, corn, and cauliflower to fill freezers for winter eating.

A New Generation of Foodies

All of these techniques made it possible for people to eat vegetables year-round before grocery stores made it easy—maybe too easy, because we forgot about the attention and work it takes to eat year-round. But people are remembering. In spite of the availability of food in grocery stores, we're in the middle of a resurgence of food preservation.

My friend Kim says it starts with jam. "You know how marijuana is the gateway drug? Jam is the gateway for food preservation. Just help people make some jam, and," she shrugged her shoulders, "you'll get hooked."

Kim and Sarah love preserving food—as in, they have a passionate, exuberant love for all things canning. Apparently, so does Ed, the apprentice who lives in our basement with his wife, Liz, who follows him into his food adventures and is quite a cook herself. They moved in at the end of August, just in time for tomatoes and pickling season. Ed saw me canning and asked me a few questions, then asked if he could borrow the canner—and later the pressure canner—and jumped into preserving. I assumed he'd done it before, diving as he did with such confidence, but he confirmed later that this was his first foray into food preservation. He was motivated by his love of local eating, access to Fern Creek's bounty and our canning equipment, and maybe the general enthusiasm about food that permeates this place. He asked a few questions, got himself Marisa McClellan's *Food in Jars*, and started canning, freezing, and dehydrating.

Kim and Sarah are both in their early thirties and busy with three small children apiece (in addition, Kim has opened her heart and home to a teenager and houses a college student besides), yet both of them manage to let food preserving take over their lives in the summer. I met them at our church's women's retreat, where we sat around tables making a collage that named things we love. One of them suggested adding "preserving food," and we started talking about salsa- and jam-making, dehydrating pears and apples, and making dandelion wine. My heart cheered.

Like Brandon and Michael—the stay-at-home dads who love the challenge and creativity of cooking—Kim and Sarah do the majority of the food preparation for their families. Their unapologetic enthusiasm for feeding their families reinforced my optimism that the world is full of hope. I invited them over for tea after the retreat to talk more about this passion they have for preserving food. They arrived bearing gifts—joy, creativity, and love in jars: rhubarb chutney, peach salsa, bread and butter pickles, relish, tomato soup, grape juice, candied jalapeños, and dandelion wine.

Both of them have been serious food preservers for about five years. Both started with jam, but around the time they had babies they got more serious about it; they wanted to feed their families well from their own hand and garden instead of paying Gerber to do it for them. One of Kim's children has life-threatening food allergies, and preserving food is one of her best ways of doing what she can to keep her children safe and healthy. She knows exactly what goes into each batch of food she cans, dehydrates, or freezes.

Kim, Sarah, and Ed talk about the deep satisfaction they get from preserving food, even if it's also a lot of work. Kim and Sarah grew up with grandmothers who filled basement shelves from ceiling to floor with home-canned goods, and Ed was motivated by a movement he saw emerging around him that was slightly nostalgic, inviting him to explore older ways of relating to food. The food security and simple goodness, the beauty of jars lined up on the counter, and a sense of industry around food preservation inspires them all. Sarah said preserving food is also an expression of her Quaker faith. She is drawn toward simplicity and toward being a good steward of land and resources—values instilled in her from childhood.

Still, not all Quakers preserve food, and three or four people do *not* a resurgence make. The reason I actually know that preserving food is resurging is the dearth of canning jars at Goodwill. I'm told they get bought up as soon as someone drops them off. Once I get over feeling like someone else took *my* jars (not very gracious or Quakerly), I can muster up some happiness about the scarcity.

Kim and Sarah see the resurgence in social media when people post pictures and recipes on Twitter, Instagram, and Facebook, thereby sanctioning food preservation as "cool" and inspiring others to come on board. While writing about food preservation trends this week, our church newsletter posted this on the Need Sheet (a virtual board where our community posts things they are looking for or have to sell): "New canners in need of supplies! We're a small group of young adults looking for canning equipment, jars of all sizes, and a food dehydrator. If you have supplies you don't need or aren't using anymore, we would love to put them to good use!"

Amazon offers further evidence. Books on food preservation have multiplied like strawberry plants, sending out runners every which way. Kim and Sarah talked about Sherri Brooks Vinton's books (she has written three in four years), whose titles all start with *Put 'em Up*! Ed, Sarah, and Kim all use *Food in Jars*. My new favorite, *Canning for a New Generation*, by Liana Krisoff (purchased after being inspired by Kim's rhubarb chutney and Sarah's candy jalapeños), is one of well over fifty books listed on Amazon about canning, many of which have been written since 2008.

This raises the question of economics. That a resurgence in food preservation would follow an economic downturn in which food security feels shaky makes all kinds of sense. If one is going to plant a garden to stave off uncertainty, one is likely going to preserve some of the abundance for later. Sarah said the choice to preserve food was related to the decision to quit her job and stay home. With more time than resources, food preservation allowed her to be resourceful and to contribute meaningfully to her family's well-being.

Both Sarah and Kim call themselves "free produce magnets." They grow a good chunk of what they preserve in their own backyards, but they also have fruit that comes from the gardens and orchards of parents and grandparents. Some of their neighbors welcome foraging and give them boxes of apples and pears, knowing they will be put to good use. Kim said that once people know you are looking for unwanted excess, they are glad to have an appreciative porch where they can drop it off. Ed and Liz can afford to buy pears, cherries, and peaches at nearby orchards, and increasing numbers of orchards and farms allow gleaning for those who cannot.

Simply put, do-it-yourself, including food preservation, is trendy. I cringe a bit at that word, but I'll take enthusiasm wherever it comes and hope that it transitions from being trendy to being an ethic that is woven into the fabric of the women and men who do it. Food is worth preserving. As are many other things.

Other Things Worth Preserving

When my kayaking friend used *fidelity* to describe my faith, she affirmed my choice to nurture and attend to a life of faith not so unlike the one passed on to me by my parents. If faith is worth preserving, so are two other virtues that Paul mentions in a letter he wrote the Corinthian church: hope and love. The greatest commandment is to love the Lord your God with all your heart, soul, and mind, and the second is like it—living out your love of God by loving your neighbor as yourself. And who is my neighbor? Jesus replied by telling the story of the Good Samaritan, a story that calls us to neighborliness: we are to love those near and far, those like us and unlike us (Luke 10:25–37).

Though it is such a strong biblical word, *love* gets overused in a sappy sort of way, so I'll join Wendell Berry in choosing *affection* to speak of it here. In his lecture "It All Turns on Affection," Berry says that in order to have a responsible relationship to the world, people must imagine their places in it. By *imagine*, Berry means to see a place fully and rightly for what it is and could be. This kind of inward and outward understanding ushers in possibilities for healing and change.

If we act out of affection, we'll think more carefully and deeply when confronted with people from storm-worn Haiti and war-torn Eastern Europe, or consumer choices that include food from pigs and cows raised in concentrated animal feeding operations and farmlands doused in petroleum-based fertilizers, herbicides, and pesticides. The alternative to acting from affection grounded in imagination and place is the application of knowledge without affection, which, Berry says, leads us astray every time.[4]

Admittedly, I am not particularly affectionate toward people I don't know, which is a point that Berry makes as well. The thousands who die in a hurricane do not matter to us nearly so much as the friend or child or spouse who dies. Since we are most deeply affected by those with whom we have a relationship, Berry argues for developing neighborliness and deep local connections to people. He argues that affection grounded in a particular place will be both broad and deep; it will include responsible love of neighbors and responsible love of the land by which a community thrives.

Still, sometimes it feels easier for me to care about children working in cocoa fields in Ghana than it is to care about my neighbor who lives next door—a neighbor I've not yet met. I can choose to only buy fair-trade chocolate and feel like I've done my duty to love my neighbor, which undoubtedly only scratches the surface. Jesus said to be neighborly to those near and far. What a peace-filled, life-flourishing world this could be if we would show affection by engaging our local and global communities in ways that tapped into our imaginations. Imagine living in a way that is rooted in an awareness of this place as God's created home, where our choices have consequences that affect neighbors, land, and the varied and brimming life in those communities.

I should take my neighbors some pickled beets and dilly beans and introduce myself. That's what Kim and Sarah would do.

In addition to faith and love, we are told to hope. My sociology students have a hard time holding on to hope when confronted with so much bad news: climate change, consumerism run amok, the global slave trade and sex trafficking, corporate crime, and rising rates of diabetes, cancers, and hunger. Still, since even a little light can dispel a lot of darkness, it's good to look for hope and light in unexpected places. Here's a tangible story of hope borne out of life on a farm.

I mostly write upstairs at an antique rolltop desk that sits by a window overlooking the garden. One day a flash of muted color zipped through the periphery of my vision, accompanied by a great squawking of our hens. I raced outside like an angry mother wanting to protect her fleeing babes from the big, beautifully colored coyote chasing them.

I ran the coyote off (which does not require the bravery those words might suggest—coyotes are skittish animals), took the dead hen out to the forest, and later, once the flock was in for the night, did a head count. We were down two and a half. The half one, Mourning, had made it back to the henhouse but was missing a chunk out of her back.

Hens don't show pain overly much, so I don't know what level of pain Mourning was experiencing, but she had a sparkle in her eye and didn't seem ready to give up on life. She huddled in a corner of the henhouse, limped when she moved, and waited to see what would happen.

What happened was that I decided to try to heal her, to have hope. To preserve her, as it were.

Mark is ever patient with ideas he thinks are a bit useless or hopeless, and he fashioned an infirmary in the corner of the henhouse. He added food and water and left the doctoring up to me.

Given my nursing background I don't freak out at the sight of trauma. That being said, I have more confidence than I should when it comes to treating things I've never encountered. I tend to think any wound can be healed, though I have been wrong as often as right.

If my only other option for treating a hen is to put her "out of her misery," I'd rather fumble my way toward giving life a chance. Nevertheless, we have killed a few injured birds rather than have them die slowly. Sometimes even I can tell when life is not going to win.

So I treated Mourning with rudimentary nursing skills that included warm water, Neosporin, 4 x 4-inch sterile pads, and nonstick tape. And compassion—mostly I treated her with compassion. To Mark's and my amazement, she healed nicely, and several months later her back feathers had grown so well they covered the scarred-over silver-dollar-size chunk of flesh missing beneath them.

Truth is, Mourning may have healed just fine on her own, but helping her out makes me a partner in this hopeful preservation process. That's good for us both. Helping something or someone other than yourself fosters hope, and that's no small thing. Birds can heal; so can land, institutions, and people. And healing doesn't always take an expert; an expert isn't always available—just people who pay attention and help out as they can.

Preservation, as I've said, takes many forms. Choices about faith, hope, and love become habits, and habits that are woven together over time form a good life. When passed on, they become gifts. Frederick Buechner says:

> Faith. Hope. Love. Those are their names of course, those three—as words so worn out, but as realities so rich. Our going-away presents from beyond time to carry with us through time to lighten our step as we go.[5]

I'm working toward choosing hope and love, trying to find hope in unexpected places, and learning to love even when it doesn't come naturally, like neighbors I've not yet met.

Preserving Life—A Community Effort

To preserve anything of importance requires obedience in the same direction. I first came across the phrase "a long obedience in the same direction" in a Eugene Peterson book by that title written thirty-five years ago. Peterson uses the Psalms of Ascent to describe fifteen characteristics of discipleship, that is, what it takes to walk in faithful obedience. Included among them are providence, worship, joy, work, happiness, perseverance, hope, humility, and community.[6] Obedience to good work, humility, and perseverance fuses with hope, worship, joy, and maybe even whimsy, when done within a community of sojourners traveling together.

Dealing with dandelions in the lawn by making wine with the flowers exhibits a kind of whimsy. Kim dons an apron of her grandmother's when she cans or makes wine or her own vanilla. She left a corporate job that sucked the life out of her and turned to teaching until she had children, and then she left teaching as well. That downwardly mobile movement brought with it redemptive soul and body health, even if she lost a society-affirming identity. Almost apologetically—fearing I might think her a bit too hippie-like (she *does* sport a tattoo on her foot)—she said getting outside in the dirt and growing things grounded her again. I showed her my tattoo, and we shared the-meaning-behind-the-tattoo stories; I told her digging in dirt grounded me, too. Kim's downwardly mobile choice brought wholeness to a life grown too dependent on convenience foods and a frenetic way of being that left little time for living, let alone thriving.

As Kim fills jars with sustenance she thinks of people from whom she has received jars, recipes, apples, and plums and prays a blessing on them. Canning is abstractly communal in this way but also rooted in tangible experience. Every year she and her grandmother make applesauce together, jars and jars of it. "I will be undone the year she is not able to do that with me," she said, though not because she isn't capable of canning on her own—most of her canning is done alone—but because canning with her grandmother has become a relationship-building, life-affirming part of their lives: two women who share a family line and affection that runs deep and wide to all those connected to it.

Canning opens the way for gracious receiving and giving as we pass on and share gifts of time, expertise, and sustenance. Sarah and Kim were inspired by their grandmothers and learned from their mothers; they have taught friends and gifted new neighbors, new parents, teachers, and people recovering from surgery and heartache with the fruits of their labor. They have accepted gifts and, in turn, gift others with intimate, personal pieces of themselves that exhibit providence, worship, joy, work, happiness, perseverance, hope, humility, and community.

They inspire me.

They've put their stamp on what this life will look like for them, which includes feeding their families and playing around with creative recipes in their kitchens. Kim is known for her dandelion wine and her rhubarb chutney, and Sarah is known for her relish, a family recipe used for three generations. Sarah's family has recently been hunting down the handwritten recipe, which gets passed from person to person; they are unsure who used it last or who has it now.

Who does that? Who borrows a handwritten recipe back and forth, year after year, rather than rewriting it to be sure it doesn't get misplaced or too splattered or dropped in a canner of boiling water? I love that they borrow it in this way, and misplace it, and find it again.

Sarah's canning community includes her mother and sister. They throw canning parties where the men take care of the children and the women give the day over to food preservation. A couple of canners bubbling on the stovetop and the popping symphony of sealing jars adds a joyous form of worship.

Their mothers and grandmothers communicated something to them that I missed, perhaps because I didn't live near either of my grandmothers and because my mother's access to food was mostly defined by whatever was available at the base commissary. Embedded into Kim and Sarah was this important value: when fruit is plentiful, preserve it in order to feed your family. A second, equally important value was also embedded: be generous.

Have I mentioned how much these two women inspire me?

Parents are generally our first instillers of values. And while I may not have received a love of preserving food from my parents, my father offered himself as a combination of whimsy, deep faith, and integrity that permeated everything he did. I am a product of his faithful obedience.

One year he pretended to be Santa Claus and scampered on the roof (he would have wanted me to add that this transpired in his pre-salvation days). He did his ho-ho-ho-ing act after we'd all gone to bed but before we would have fallen into dreams of dancing sugarplums. Some years later (post-salvation) I snapped a picture, which is still anchored with photo corners in an old album. It's a black-and-white photograph of Dad sporting my 1969 glasses while holding our too-big-to-be-a-lapdog in his lap (Dragon Lady was none too happy about this turn of events). He is squinting through my glasses and waving like a girl. I think he was pretending to be me. Maybe thirty years later, as he was dying of a cancer that he fought valiantly, he told me he'd meet me by the middle north gate in heaven. Whimsy with deep faith braided into the fabric—that was Dad to the end.

I'm also grateful for my mother, who shapes me still. She taught me how to make *blina* and cultivated in me a love of German foods and the confidence to cook with and without recipes. She'd rip out my seams in junior high when I made unforgiving mistakes in my efforts to sew. I would have quit straight up without her beside me, willing to carry that part of my burden. I remembered that one day when I found myself doing the same for my daughter, a gift learned and passed down from my mother.

The keeping of anything worth saving takes collective effort. Preservation requires a community to carry values and skills forward, light the way, cheer us on, keep us laughing and hopeful and humble, and guide us back toward the path when we lose our way.

I'll share one more story, which came from Nathan—a man Mark knows and whom I have never met. Nathan heard about my project and told Mark this preservation story about making apple butter and giving me permission to share it. Even though I only share the end of the story here, it is full of goodness.

> I love autumn, partly because of the canning and preserving we did with apples. More so than even Christmas or Thanksgiving my extended family would come together and produce something so fine. My grandfather had a large part in raising me and I studied him during those times—imitating his movements and watching everything he did. During these gatherings he taught me to call crows using grass blades and skip rocks and whistle with my thumb and ring finger. As our family has aged, broken apart, or dwindled, coming together for these weekends has provided constancy and familiarity. We grieved my mother's absence last year—but we made apple butter (in some ways) to honor her memory and the memories of my grandfather and others. I look forward to carrying on the tradition with my children.[7]

Preserving Faith: A Brief Reprise

I used to think conversion happened at some moment in time when one stepped from darkness into light and stopped being lost. Now I think of conversion as a journey—whether a conversion of faith or a conversion to a different way of living. In either case, but especially in the first, it is less about making our way toward God and more about maintaining a willingness to be carried along in a river that *is* God. God carries us, as it were, and persevering requires the choice to stay attentive and to float, to leave off our impulse to paddle more times than not.

When Henri Nouwen says he resists choosing God, I relate well. I do not choose to be open to God every moment, to be attentive, to stop paddling my way frenetically forward toward God—or God knows where. How hard it is to rest in God so that I can pay attention to all God gives me to see.

Nouwen writes:

A life of faith is a life of gratitude—it means a life in which I am willing to experience my complete dependence upon God and to praise and thank him unceasingly for the gift of being. A truly eucharistic life means always saying thanks to God, always praising God, and always being more surprised by the abundance of God's goodness and love. How can such a life not also be a joyful life? It is the truly converted life in which God has become the center of all. There gratitude is joy and joy is gratitude and everything becomes a surprising sign of God's presence.[8]

When I give myself over to complete dependence on God and become attentively filled with gratitude, the changing landscapes of life come alive. I marvel at the beauty of women enthusiastically preserving food for their families; weep at the destruction of war, disease, and humanity's abuse of God's earth; and am astonished and filled with gratitude when I see destruction healed with time, compassion, and the participation of human hands doing the work of God.

Obedience means letting go enough to pay attention. Affection for fellow kayakers in the river wells up in an obedient soul and gets woven into affection for God. Love of the willow trees—and deer near the bank—drinking deeply from the river wells up because they are part of the world that God loves. Could gratitude and joy flow any more easily out of such a life?

Preserving what God loves is less complicated when I don't feel responsible to fix the world but rather choose to attend to it and love it as God does. This paying attention, this loving gratitude, is my long obedience.

Still, releasing myself to live with so light a burden is difficult when I more habitually understand obedience as an achievement that gives me something to show for my efforts. But paying attention and falling in love is no small thing. Ripples form and follow kayaks (and ducks!) as they move through water. Perhaps if we looked we'd see the ripples from our God-carried kayaks touching other kayakers and eventually lapping the shores. Maybe those gratitude- and love-filled ripples change the world more than we imagine.

A Starter Guide to Food Preservation

Moving back and forth between preserving faith and preserving food might feel dizzying, like walking from starboard to port on a small ship in a choppy sea. Maybe the jarring effect of my shifting focus says something about a disconnect between food and faith. As communion makes sacred the earthy tangible truth that we eat in order to live, perhaps food preservation can remind us not only of our capacity to preserve that which fosters life but also God's faithful, persistent love and preservation of life.

Can our senses awaken to God's sustaining grace through hearty chili made from food preserved and brought together in a dish that warms us to the bone? Imagine earthy Black Turtle and Calypso beans marrying with canned tomatoes and tomato sauce (once sun-kissed), frozen corn seasoned with sautéed onions and garlic, dried peppers and/or chili powder, salt and pepper, a bit of honey, and a splash of balsamic vinegar. Eating preserved foods blended together on a cold winter night (served with cornbread sweetened with August honey from the bees), we taste the hope-filled promise that spring will return and that we will be fed through to the next harvest.

Toward that hope-filled experience here is a starter guide to food preservation. For a more in-depth account of all these methods, I recommend Sherri Brooks Vinton's home preservation book, *Put 'em Up!*. Mostly, I'm whetting your appetite to play with food, get creative, and taste and see that the Lord is good.

For those who have tried food preservation and given up because something went awry, think of me as your mother ripping out seams in a garment so you can try your hand again at something you've felt inadequately skilled to accomplish. For those who have never tried at all, borrow my confidence that anyone with a freezer and a rubber band can dry some herbs and freeze some berries to eat when winter comes.

Don't be daunted by the time required. Preserving can take a few minutes (tying up herbs) or fifteen to twenty minutes (blanching beans and freezing them on a tray) or an afternoon (making and canning tomato sauce). I tend to do a bit here and there, in one- or two-hour chunks. Kim and Sarah give many summer evenings over to it, being as they are preserving on a grand scale and preparing salsas, jams, and chutneys as part of the process. Sarah reminds us that one can throw an all-day party with other canners and preserve a varied bounty of goodness in the company of friends.

In all cases choose fruit and vegetables that are fresh and in good condition—like what we'd expect of any virtue, value, or belief worth hanging on to; if it's good, it's worth preserving.

Dehydrating Herbs, Fruits, and Tomatoes

Dehydrating foods removes the moisture that bacteria need to grow and slows down the enzymes in food that eventually carry it back to dirt. That means dehydrated food can last a long time—more than a year. Still, it will deteriorate over time, so try to use everything up within the year.

Equipment needed: for herbs, a bit of string or rubber bands. Fruits and tomatoes *could* be dried on a rock in a hot sun, but using an oven on the lowest heat setting possible (not very energy efficient, but it works) or a food dehydrator (which is worth purchasing new or used) speeds up the process.

Vegetables and Fruit

Slice tomatoes, zucchini, pears, and apples into ⅜-inch slices, cut strawberries in half (or ¼-inch slices), and dry peas and blueberries whole. Cut large grapes and cherry tomatoes in half or be prepared for a very long drying time. Arrange fruits in a single layer on stackable food dehydrator screens. When possible place berries, grapes, or tomatoes with the cut side up to prevent them from dripping on trays below. Dehydrate at a temperature between 125 and 135 degrees and rotate trays throughout the drying process (every four hours or so). Dehydrating will take anywhere from five to fourteen hours, depending on how much water is in the fruit or vegetable, how thickly they have been sliced, and how thoroughly dehydrated you want them. I start pulling off smaller pieces when the fruit reaches the chewiness of raisins (taste testing more than a few, which I excuse as a need to check for doneness). Mushy fruit will mildew. If pieces get overly dry and are cut very thin, they will be crunchy, or if cut thicker, they will be tough and quite chewy. As such, they are best added to simmering oatmeal to soften them up. Any fruit or vegetable can be rehydrated and used in cooking, but generally we snack on ours—except tomatoes, which I toss into soups, pasta dishes, and casseroles when I want to punch up the tomato flavor. Dehydrated

fruit does not need to be kept in the freezer, since dehydrating it preserves it adequately. However, do store it in jars with tight-fitting lids in
a cool, dark place.

Herbs

Create a bunch/bundle and tie it with string or wrap it with a rubber
band. Hang bundles on a string in the kitchen (paper clips make nice hooks)
or in a laundry room or pantry or just about anywhere until the leaves are
dry and brittle. Remove the leaves over a cookie sheet with edges to contain
the inevitable scattering of leaves, and then store the herbs in glass jars.
For maximum flavor, wait to crush or crumble leaves until cooking with
them. Replace herbs annually with the next year's crop.

Freezing Fruits and Vegetables

Equipment needed: freezer space, baking trays, freezer bags or glass jars
with wide or extra-wide mouths. In addition, you may sometimes need a
big pot, a bowl, and a slotted spoon. Freezing requires very little time and
no special equipment. We freeze berries and use them in our oatmeal, as
well as for pies, cobblers, and smoothies all winter long. Most fruit and
vegetables are best used within six months, though my goal is generally
to use them before the next flush of new fresh food.

Fruit

Berries you've picked yourself and know haven't been contaminated
with sprays or fumes or other undesirables can be frozen without being
washed. If you aren't sure, rinse and pat berries dry. Freeze berries in a
single layer on cookie sheets for a couple of hours; once frozen, separate
those that are stuck together and store in freezer bags, glass jars, or wax-
lined cardboard boxes.

Vegetables

Unlike fruit, vegetables need to be blanched before freezing to stop
the enzymes that would otherwise keep them ripening and render them
tasteless at the other end.

Blanching with boiling water. Use a gallon of water for every pound of vegetables and blanch in batches. Bring the water to a boil, drop in a pound of washed and trimmed (if appropriate) vegetables, bring back to a boil, and boil approximately one and a half to three minutes (the lesser amount for smaller or less substantial vegetables like chard, about two minutes for peas and corn, and three for broccoli and beans). If you have a colander or basket that fits into a pan, use it to lower and lift vegetables all at once; otherwise, use as big a slotted spoon or ladle as you have or can find at Goodwill to lift out the vegetables so that you can use the same water for other batches.

Blanching with steam. In this case water is boiling beneath the vegetables, and the steam does the blanching. A pot with an inserted basket or tray sits above the water steaming the vegetables. Add about one-and-a-half times the length of minutes it takes to blanch with boiling water. Add the vegetables once the water is boiling, cover with a lid, and start timing.

For both boiling and steaming, immediately transfer vegetables from the

❧ *A Word about Glass vs. Plastic* ❧

If I could, I'd eliminate all plastic bags and containers intended to store food from my kitchen. Here's why:

1. Years ago I heard that we shouldn't microwave food in plastic. That advice is being taken seriously now, along with advice about not leaving plastic bottles of liquid in the sun. There are questions about the safety of storing food in plastic. It seems intuitive to me now; plastic is a petroleum product, after all. In 2008, alarm bells went off with studies suggesting a link between BPA (bisphenol A, a chemical that has been used to harden plastic since the late 1950s) and health problems like cancers and heart, brain, and behavior problems. We all have BPA in our bodies by this time because most of us have eaten food stored in plastic over the course of our lives. Still, less is better, and none is better yet. BPA-free plastic is supposed to be the safe alternative, and parents have been counting on that, although a 2011 study suggests that BPA-free plastics are not problem free—leaching still happened in the 455 common plastics

heat to a prepared bowl of ice water and let them cool down. Replenish the ice water as needed if doing multiple batches.

Drain well and freeze immediately. To be able to separate pieces later, freeze them on a cookie sheet first. I do this for peas, beans, corn, and broccoli, which I guess is just about everything except chard and spinach.

Winter squash can be baked or steamed and the meat scooped out and frozen in one- to two-cup batches for later use in soups, breads, and desserts. A root cellar or a spare unheated bedroom will keep raw, whole squash throughout the winter. For the most part, I freeze whatever portion of a squash I've baked up but not used.

Herbs

Herbs and onions are frozen without blanching, though I prefer drying herbs and keeping onions in the root cellar. Follow the directions for fruit,

tested.[9] I'd rather not store food in a container made out of something that would be toxic to consume in its raw state and appears to leach. Why take unnecessary risks with avoidable carcinogenic, heart- and mind-disturbing plastics? When I buy dry foods in plastic bags (lentils, popcorn, bulk foods), I transfer them to glass when I get them home. Leftovers go into canning jars. But alas, this week I realized I still have ketchup and mustard in plastic bottles, and anytime I buy yogurt, sour cream, ricotta, or any number of other dairy items, they only come in plastic containers. I'm eradicating what I can.

2. Plastic does not break down in a landfill like glass, metal, cardboard, and paper, so it is not a sustainable, earth-friendly product. I recycle what I can (e.g., yogurt containers) but try to buy milk, peanut butter, spice containers, and anything that gives me an option in glass or waxed cardboard rather than plastic.

3. I want my kitchen to look like my grandma's, and her pantry shelves and refrigerator weren't full of plastic. While my pining for her kitchen might be borne from romanticizing her life, it still calls me to a more simple and sustainable one. Filled glass jars are beautiful, and aesthetics matter.

chopping or slicing the onions however preferred. Extra cilantro or ginger that won't be used before it wilts or goes soft can be frozen. Put directly into a glass jar or bag. The cilantro will be "wilted" when thawed, so it works best when sautéed or cooked or blended in a dressing.

Canning Fruits, Pickles, and Jams

Equipment needed: canner with wire jar holder or stockpot, canning jars, lids/rings. Other tools are helpful but not necessary (e.g., a wide funnel for filling jars and canning tongs for lifting hot jars out of the canner). Wouldn't it be great if neighbors shared equipment and churches had lending libraries for garden and canning tools as well as for books?

Water-bath canning preserves food by destroying enzymes that naturally decompose produce and microorganisms that make it unsafe to eat. By boiling jars full of food with lids that can seal, an airless vacuum is created that pushes vapors out. The jars seal as they cool, and microorganisms can't survive in an environment without oxygen. Canned foods can last more than a year, but unlike wine, the flavor doesn't grow more interesting with time; it's best used or given away in time for the next season's bounty.

The basic task is to wash and trim fresh produce, put it into clean jars, and process or can it. More specifically, put empty clean jars in a canner or stockpot that is between one-half and two-thirds full of water. As the water heats up, it will semisterilize and warm them. Remove the jars when the produce has been prepped, fill the jars, and add hot water (in some cases brine) to between one-half inch and one inch of the top. In some cases salt and/or lemon juice or vinegar will be added. Jiggle the jar or run a knife down the sides to get rid of bubbles, wipe the rim, and screw on the lid. Place jar in the canner/stock pot with simmering water that covers it by a good inch or two and boil for a prescribed amount of time. Remove and allow to sit undisturbed on the counter for twelve hours. The jars will play their one-note song as each of them seals during the cooling process. Sometimes two or three jars pop close together; sometimes they are separated by an hour or so. After twelve hours, check to see that each jar has sealed by pressing down on the center. If a lid pops down and back up it isn't sealed; put these jars in the refrigerator and use them first. Remove the rings; rinse and store them. Store your jars out of direct sunlight. Water-bath canning is very simple and a creative way to preserve food for later.

The National Center for Home Food Preservation offers everything anyone needs to know about canning times for various vegetables and fruits, how to change it up given your altitude, and which produce can and cannot be canned in a water bath with confidence. Check out their information at nchfp.uga.edu/how/can_home.html.

Pressure Cooking

Fruits, jams, and all things pickled can be preserved with a water-bath canner. Foods low in acid, including most vegetables, need another line of defense to be safely preserved. Pressure does what heat alone cannot do: it kills harmful bacteria that could survive water-bath canning. Rather than go into detail about pressure canning here, I recommend you find someone who has done it before to offer hands-on guidance.

If a growing season is still some ways off, whet your appetite by going to the library or a bookstore and browsing books on canning. Many are beautiful and nearly all of them inspiring.

• *McMurray Salsa* •

This is Kim's adaptation of a recipe from her cousin, which is based on her mother-in-law's recipe.

8–10	tomatoes (with skins)
2	large yellow onions
4–5	mild bell peppers
3	hot peppers (jalapeño)
2 tbsp.	cilantro
2	cloves garlic, minced
½ c.	vinegar
12 oz.	tomato paste
1 tbsp.	salt

| 1 tbsp. | chili powder |
| ½ tsp. | oregano |

Chop veggies. Combine the chopped veggies, vinegar, tomato paste, and spices in a large, nonreactive pot. Bring to a boil and cook over medium heat for 30 minutes.

To Preserve
Use the water-bath method. Ladle into clean, hot canning jars, leaving ½ inch of headspace. Release trapped air, wipe the rims clean, and screw on jar bands. Process 15 minutes.

Reflections and Questions

1. Henri Nouwen's quote at the beginning of the chapter is about choosing God's thoughts, words, and actions and the difficulty of doing so. Reflect on or journal about places in your life where you resist choosing God and where you do choose God.

2. Preservation takes many forms. What are some "hope-filled flourishing" things (like faith, hobbies, habits, virtues, or relationships) that you are faithful to and preserve? Do you have habits that are destructive to you and those around you? What might it mean to choose God in these contexts?

3. This chapter gives a nostalgic history lesson about food—specifically, food preservation. Does it spark your interest in preserving food? If so, how?

4. In Wendell Berry's address "It All Turns on Affection," he says that in order to have a responsible relationship to the world people must imagine their places in it, which means to see a place fully and rightly for what it is and could be. How might you imagine your place in the world and see the place itself more fully? What might acting out of love or affection look like as you choose God by loving neighbors who live in particular places, both close to you and far away?

5. The chapter suggests that our faith journey may be less about making our way to God and more about being willing to be carried, to stay attentive, and to float, leaving off the impulse to paddle our way toward God. How has being carried characterized your faith journey?

Perhaps this idea of preserving faith by choosing to stay attentive while being carried challenges you. If so, reflect on that.

6. If you are new to food preservation, what is one food that you think you could preserve easily enough after reading this chapter? If you are not new to food preservation, what is one new thing you might try—either a technique, a food, or perhaps an invitation to someone unfamiliar with food preservation to join you in a preservation adventure?

4

Eating Closer to Home

On Being Neighborly

> Our life and death depend upon our relationship with our neighbor. If we gain our neighbor, we have gained God. If we offend our neighbor, we have sinned against Christ.
>
> —Abba Anthony[1]

The dandelions awoke on a sunny day near the end of March, following on the heels of a month's worth of rain that fell in three days' time. Bright yellow flowers opened to the sun, welcoming bees and other insects looking for pollen and nectar, and welcoming a giant forager eager for blossoms to make dandelion wine. "Pick me!" they seemed to say. So I did, knowing more would come. Aware of my fellow harvesters, I waited to pick a blossom until a hardworking bee took off for another blossom or for home, hind legs heavily laden with yellow pollen.

Kim and Sarah came to pick up our surplus strawberry plants, a nice by-product of pruning baby strawberry plants, which multiply like rabbits. They were the last of the community supported agriculture (CSA) members, friends, and family who came to pick up plants to start or embellish their own strawberry patches. While Kim was there, I committed to her that I would take the step (sigh) to welcome my new neighbors before starting to brew any dandelion nectar. Committing gave me a deadline and a witness. Elsewise, I knew that I might never make it up to my neighbor's front door, in spite of my best intentions. (Do you find it odd, dear reader, that it is so much easier for me to write a book for an unknown audience than to go meet a neighbor I might have to look in the eye?)

With bolstered courage and a belief that gracious hospitality can still happen in this part of the world (inspired as I was by Kim and Sarah), I walked up our neighbors' long driveway on a Sunday afternoon carrying a purple paper bag that held a quart of jalapeño dilly beans, a pint of pickled beets, five yellow Cortland onions still firm and succulent from the last summer's harvest, and a note welcoming our neighbors to the neighborhood. On my way up the driveway I second-guessed myself. Home-canned goods are a risky gift, after all. They may not like their pickles hot or beets in any form. They may throw it all away once I'm gone, not knowing me well enough to know whether or not my food would make them sick.

Their driveway weaves between a dappled forest with enough sun breaking through to sustain a floor of ferns, and I felt welcome in it, even if unsure of what awaited me at the end of the driveway. As I walked, I reminded myself that these neighbors are my local folk, and I want to be neighborly. Obediently neighborly.

Love Your Neighbor as Yourself

For most of my life, being neighborly has felt optional—nice, but not necessary.

That notion was dispelled while visiting a HNGR (Human Needs Global Resources) intern in Malawi as part of a program I participated in as a professor at Wheaton College. As an adviser I'd spend five or six days with my students halfway through their six-month internship, which involved living and working in a majority world (what used to be called the developing world) country—far-off places like Indonesia, Bolivia, Peru, and Uganda. Advisers went to advise but also to help students work through snags related to the internship, their living arrangements, or emotional/spiritual/interpersonal needs. During these one-on-one visits, the students became the guides, and the advisers became the students as the interns led us around their extraordinary lives. Gracious hospitality abounded everywhere I went; it poured out from internship supervisors, hosting families, and my students.

During my visit to Malawi I sat in on the morning devotions led by Sandress Msiska, a theologian and the country director of World Relief. He talked about Jesus's response to the question, "What is the greatest commandment?"

> "Love the Lord your God with all your heart and with all your soul and with all your mind." This is the first and greatest commandment. And the second is like it: "Love your neighbor as yourself." All the Law and the Prophets hang on these two commandments. (Matt. 22:37–40 NIV)

Loving our neighbor is how we love God, said Msiska. The second commandment is equally important as the first; it is the flesh and blood of loving God. We love an intangible God by loving our tangible neighbor. We extend compassion, justice, and mercy to anyone in need because, as Jesus affirms with the story of the Good Samaritan, everyone and anyone is our neighbor.

So much for neighborliness being optional.

Astronaut Russell Schweickart, in an essay published in 1983, tries to use words to capture his experience as the lunar module pilot of the Apollo 9 mission. Every ninety minutes he orbited the Earth and later described how precious the whole of it became, how he came to identify with the Middle East and Africa and Asia. He wanted the warring factions to see what he saw—that visible boundaries don't exist from the vantage point of space, how the whole of the Earth hangs in an immense space that, from the distance of the moon, can be blotted out with a thumb. Schweickart ends the essay this way:

> You realize that on that small spot, that little blue and white thing, is everything that means anything to you—all love, tears, joy, games, all of it on that little spot out there. . . . It's a feeling that says you have a responsibility. . . . There's a difference in that relationship between you and that planet, and all those other forms of life on that planet, because you've had that kind of experience. It's a difference and it's so precious.[2]

Our neighborhoods are both immense and small. We experience the smallness with neighbors who sleep, eat, fight, and play next door. They are the messiest to love because we share fences and blowing weed seeds, obnoxious noises drifting from garages and backyards late in the night, and unfamiliar—or *too* familiar—smells wafting through high-rise apartment complexes. But sometimes we exchange extra apples from the apple tree, car rides, help in time of trouble, or the proverbial cup of sugar.

Being the social creatures that we are, we tend to cluster with people like us. We find it easiest to be neighborly toward people who share our religious beliefs or social and ethnic class, people who do similar kinds of work and recreation, or those who hold similar political views. Sometimes we are neighborly beyond this "sameness." In the context of church families or extended families replete with difference, we remain in relationship in spite of (sometimes because of) that difference. The common denominator of worshiping together can transcend differences just as familial bonds can help us seek out ways to be gracious to one another in spite of sometimes significant dissimilarities.

We also manage to be neighborly toward people we do not know through the taxes we pay and donations we choose to make. In my less-hospitable moments, I'd like to imagine that my obligation to be neighborly gets met in all these ways so that I don't have to be particularly mindful toward any *particular* neighbors.

Still, I wonder whether Schweickart's words are a nudge for us to expand our neighborhood, allowing relationships with other members of this planet to become, as he says, deeply precious. As Abba Anthony puts it, "Our life and death depend upon our relationship with our neighbor. If we gain our neighbor, we have gained God. If we offend our neighbor, we have sinned against Christ." This is not unlike what Msiska said and is perhaps mirrored in the reflections of Schweickart from space: we love God by loving our neighbors—and *all* members of creation qualify as our neighbor to some degree.

The truth is, living into neighborly commitments is in our best interest. As my neighbors flourish, so will I. We are inextricably linked in an interdependent relationship. I sometimes act as though this reality does not exist, as though I can flourish if the ecosystems that feed me become crippled and die, as though I may not be called on to share my spot on earth with people whose homes are being overtaken by expanding deserts or rising seas. My neighborhood is, after all, rather large, and being neighborly can feel overwhelming.

It helps me to recognize that eating gives me daily opportunities to love my neighbors. That seems doable enough. But still, it takes intention to eat in neighborly ways; it used to be less complicated. Allow me to join others in making an audacious claim: the green revolution, which I referred to earlier as the *so-called* green revolution, is the biggest single cause of our food woes and contributes greatly to global injustices and misery.

Is calling out a revolution that helped feed a billion people who might have otherwise starved grossly insensitive? Perhaps. But seventy-five years later, we are witnessing the unintended consequences of a revolution that morphed into a global agribusiness that puts profit before people. In the process of pushing more corn, wheat, soy, and rice out of every field, we justified or overlooked the fact that we were also wreaking havoc on the planet and its inhabitants. Might this global industrial food system alienate us from our relationship to God's verdant garden and from our neighbors in ways that not only allow invisible injustices to abound but also devastate the ecosystems that feed us?

A fairly well-accepted idea is that the only way to feed the masses is through a global food industry (even if it is unfortunately marked by injustice and misery) that alienates us from each other and our places and leads to confusion about what is healthy for our bodies, our communities, and our world.

Vandana Shiva, a physicist and international environmental activist, addressed a group of 1,200 people who were gathered for a Cultivate Kansas City conference.[3] Shiva says, "For a short time the mechanistic mind has projected onto the world the false idea that food production is and must be of necessity an industrial activity. That's a world view that is in profound error." She unpacks her thoughts on this matter before embracing the hopeful change provided by the local food movement, which is based on making good, wholesome food available to one's local community rather than based on acquiring wealth at the expense of the well-being of individuals, local communities, and, particularly for Shiva, our planet. Shiva says, "It's all about love, about bestowing attention, fostering, cherishing, honoring, tending, guarding, and loving the Earth which provides our food."[4]

The Brown Tinge of the Green Revolution

Shiva joins Wendell Berry, Michael Pollan, and other prominent voices heralding the need to bring affection, or love, back into the conversation about how we grow our food. Norman Wirzba sees our distorted relationship with our food system as a result of being a people in exile:

> To be in exile marks an inability to live peaceably, sustainably, and joyfully in one's place. Not knowing or loving *where* we are and *who* we are with, we don't know *how* to live in ways that foster mutual flourishing and delight. More specifically, we don't know how *through our eating* to live sympathetically into the memberships that make creation a life-giving home.[5]

Wirzba blames our exile on the green revolution. But to be fair, the green revolution was born out of a desire and hope to find a way to feed a population on the cusp of exploding. Initially, that goal was accomplished. Through a combination of modern agricultural practices that went global—the adoption of tractors, irrigation systems, hybridized seeds that produced heftier crops, synthetic fertilizers that pushed soil fertility, and pesticides and herbicides that combated pests and weeds—we grew more food.

Norman Borlaug won the Nobel Peace Prize in 1970 and is credited both with saving the lives of those billion starving people and bringing world peace by increasing the global food supply (though the world peace was rather short-lived). While the hopes and intentions that he represented were noble, the costs and natural limits of industrial agriculture weren't adequately considered.

We built a global food system dependent on fossil fuel to run tractors, to transport food, and to make pesticides, herbicides, and fertilizers. Even if burning fossil fuel had no negative effect on the atmosphere, petroleum is a limited resource. It comes from fossils, after all, which aren't made in a year—or even a lifetime or millennia.

An unanticipated cost of industrialized food (and more broadly, industrialization) is our global climate-change crises. All that CO_2 (carbon dioxide) held secure in fossils and forests for all those years is being released into and then trapped by the atmosphere. Agricultural practice and deforestation are the two single biggest causes for increased heat-trapping gases. We chop down forests not only for lumber and paper but also to clear space for planting grains and palm trees, or for banana, cocoa, or coffee plantations. It's like turning up the heat of an electric blanket in order to keep warm, even though turning up the temperature causes an assortment of overheating problems.[6] We have caused expanding dead zones in oceans where no fish, coral reefs, or other ocean life exists or can exist; growing areas of eroding and depleted soil around the globe; water depletion and expanding deserts; the flooding of coastal areas and islands; and the pollution of rivers and lakes from the toxic runoff of industry and agribusiness.

This certainly sounds like a dreary and hopeless tale. Skeptics call it "far-fetched," but most geologists, climatologists, and other earth scientists who have looked into the matter agree that a global food system dependent on fossil fuel is unsustainable. A groundswell of folks manifest their hope that a local food movement can be a way forward—like the seven hundred small-scale farmers that come to Oregon State's Small Farms Conference every year, or the 1,200 who showed up for Cultivate Kansas City, or the thousands involved in food webs in counties across the nation, and the tens of thousands more who belong to CSAs and community gardens and shop at farmers markets. Add to that the politicians and pastors, county commissioners, and city planners working toward healthier people, healthier communities, and a healthier world, and we've born ourselves a movement.

There is always hope. The sustaining presence of God ensures it. Hope bubbles forth in corporate boardrooms, state capitals, and international assemblies. But it's also simmering in homes, neighborhoods, and communities. Hope-filled change can start with anyone who chooses to eat food grown and raised closer to home.

Global Eating: Home Kitchen Considerations

Imagine drawing up a shopping list for a summer party, keeping in mind the complication of trying to be a good global neighbor. Let's have a hypothetical conversation in which I'll anticipate and then answer some questions related to planning the party. Then I'll offer some simple suggestions for ways to eat more neighborly.

I want to be extravagant with my food plans for this party. Is that irresponsible?

Perhaps we ought to consider the question beneath this question: "Is there enough food for everyone, and does my extravagance matter?" Yes. And yes.

Even before the 1970s' global food crisis, people in wealthy countries have been asking this question—*Is there enough food for everyone?* That's what motivated the green revolution. Yes, there *could* be enough food, but those of us in wealthy countries need to eat a bit differently than we do to lower the demand we place on the world for our food. Lowering our demand gives others more breathing space to grow food for their own communities and farming sovereignty to people in the Global South,[7] where the vast majority of humanity lives.

The Earth Policy Institute, a nonprofit environmental organization, studies and analyzes environmental factors. They make policy and lifestyle recommendations to promote health for the planet and people in economically sustainable ways. In an effort to spread the word, the Earth Policy Institute makes all their research and recommendations available free online and in books and reports,[8] which seems pretty neighborly to me. In one report, Lester Brown summarizes global diets and food availability and concludes that if everyone ate like we do in the United States, the world could sustain 2.5 billion people well. If we all ate like they do in Italy (more vegetables and grains, less meat), the world could sustain 5 billion people well. If we all ate like they do in India (a plant-based diet), the earth could feed 10 billion people well. The world population is about 7.3 billion.

The explanation is more complicated, and Brown goes into that. It's based on how much grain is needed for good nutrition and whether or not that grain is eaten directly or first fed to animals that people then eat.

A second part of the question about whether or not there's enough food has to do with food waste, the amount of which suggests that plenty of food is being grown but a lot of it never makes it to anyone's table. Wealthy nations tend to waste a lot of food.

In the United Kingdom, 40 percent of fresh fish purchased at supermarkets is thrown away before it is eaten, along with 23 percent of eggs, and 20 percent of milk.[9] We throw so much away in part because we pay attention to conservative use-by or best-used-by dates, as though we will get sick or die if we do not. If the date stamped on the box, carton, or bag has passed (or is within a day or two of passing), those of us who can afford to do so tend to toss it rather than "risk it." Unless we are talking about sliced meats (which I'd toss rather than risk), most of that food is fine beyond the use-by date. Some types of food will lose flavor and texture, but even that can be repurposed.

I imagine my grandma pulled milk from the fridge that had been there a while, looked at it, smelled it, tasted it, and *then* decided whether to serve it to her family or bake it up in a cake. Most use-by and best-used-by dates are determined at the discretion of manufacturers. They help avoid litigation or a bad reputation over something like soured milk, and they encourage consumers to buy more because they toss more.

Smell is a good way to determine whether milk has curdled in the refrigerator and soured. One could, like Grandma, use soured milk in place of buttermilk for pancakes or cornbread. Eggs will keep in the refrigerator between four and six months, in spite of dates to the contrary. Wilted vegetables can be tossed in soups and stir-fries, and wrinkled apples are delicious baked into crumbles or crisps or made into applesauce.

People in wealthy nations can afford to throw food away because we spend only about 10 percent of our income on food, unlike people in India, who spend a quarter of their income on food. And since we pay less for it, we value it less.

But a lot of food, particularly produce, never even makes it from the field to the supermarket. The market's standards of produce perfection mean that imperfect apples, cucumbers, carrots, and potatoes are tossed. A lot of what we harvest at Fern Creek wouldn't meet the industry standards of perfection required today. All farmers have this problem. The solution? Overplant to ensure enough near-perfect produce to sell. The rest can be composted, which isn't a *bad* thing, but it's not particularly a good thing either, especially when we are looking at food shortages. In the European Union, close to 50 percent of crops grown never make it to the supermarkets. Pesticides, herbicides, and fertilizers (where they are used) are also wasted, along with water that irrigates crops that never make it to market.

So yes, feast away on special days, but do so in responsible ways. In *Eat with Joy*, Rachel Marie Stone talks about the difference between ferial (ordinary) and festal (feast) eating. When our ordinary days always include what used to be reserved for celebrations, then we really have to go over the top to create a feast. Stone says of her family:

> We don't eat desserts most days, which heightens the uniqueness and special-ness of birthdays, when we eat cake. Because we eat a lot of simple foods—beans and rice, vegetarian stews, soup and bread—a nice beef stew can be a celebration meal. It's actually freeing to orient yourself toward a festal-ferial approach to food. It frees you from feeling that every eating occasion must be celebration-worthy, and it frees you to exercise your culinary creativity for days of true celebration.[10]

While you ponder that, I'll propose another hypothetical question:

I was thinking of hosting a surf-and-turf sort of barbecue, which we hardly ever do. But I hear that seafood costs a lot to ship, and shipping food long distances is bad for the environment. So, unless I'm visiting a coastline, is a surf-and-turf barbeque irresponsible? Should I never eat seafood if I live somewhere like Nebraska?

I'm an hour away from the Pacific Ocean, and local fish is fairly easy to come by (though not free of controversy), so it's easy for me to say save the surf feasting for when you are visiting a coast and otherwise experiment with local trout, catfish, and bass. Lest that sound too austere for lobster lovers, go ahead and host a surf-and-turf celebration on a special occasion and enjoy the extravagance. But know that it *is* an extravagance and celebrate mindfully—and infrequently.

As a fan of the backstory, allow me to enumerate some of those hidden costs that follow us into our kitchens, pantries, and grills.

I mentioned earlier that since the Industrial Revolution we have increasingly shuffled food around the world. We import cocoa from Ghana, coffee from Guatemala, and rice from China. Some of this makes sense. It can be neighborly to buy each other's produce, especially when we can't grow it ourselves. We grow most of the rice consumed in the United States in Louisiana, California, Texas, and Arkansas, but it takes a lot of water to grow rice—and water is increasingly hard to come by in those southern states. Getting rice from countries where water abounds makes sense. It is neighborly; though theoretically, if we don't have a good relationship with our neighbors, they might stop selling rice to us. This fear motivates countries to secure a local food supply, prompting them to grow their own rice.

But cocoa, coffee, pineapple, mangoes, and bananas only grow near the equator. No matter how much we plead with the soil and sun, we can't get them to grow in North America. So if we want chocolate and bananas to be part of our diet, we have to buy them from our neighbors, which we can do in neighborly ways.

We also move a lot of food around that grows in our backyards, just not year-round. We've come to like fresh tomatoes, cucumbers, strawberries, and bell peppers *all the time*. If it grows in July we want it available in January. That means produce has to be put on a truck, boat, or plane to get from warmer central and southern climates to cooler northern ones.

Sometimes the reasons why we move food to and fro make even less sense than simply wanting cantaloupe in February. Corn grown in South America gets shipped to feed cows raised in Europe that will be consumed by people in the United States and Canada. Europe could grow its own corn, but it costs more to grow it in Europe than to buy it from South America. Nearly half of the fresh fruit we eat in the United States is imported, even though we grow a lot of fruit here. For instance, we are second only to

China in apple production. Speaking of apples, in 2012 the United States exported nearly two billion pounds of them to places like Taiwan, Hong Kong, and India. But at the same time we import nearly half a billion pounds from places like Chili and New Zealand.[11]

Isn't that crazy? The left hand (exports) does not know what the right hand (imports) is doing and, frankly, doesn't give a rip. It makes sense economically or it wouldn't happen. But it wouldn't make sense if the environmental costs of burning all that fossil fuel were factored into the spreadsheet.

So maybe it's not surprising that the average plate of food in the United States travels between 1,200 and 1,500 miles to get from farm to table, although I still find that rather shocking, mostly because a good chunk of Mark's and my food comes from our backyard. An Iowa State University study tracked the origins of food arriving at the Chicago Terminal in 1981, 1990, and 1998. By 1998, food coming into Chicago had traveled approximately 1,500 miles, an increase of 250 miles since 1981. During the same year an average plate of local food traveled 44.5 miles.[12] All those miles make enough cents to offset how little sense it makes otherwise.

Meat has hidden costs, too. Grain is grown one place and transported to another place to feed steers, which are transported from wherever they were born to a feedlot somewhere and then sold and transported to where they will be slaughtered and processed and then trucked or shipped to wherever the beef will be sold.

Unsurprisingly, the human activity that contributes the most to climate change involves food. Growing food for people, growing food for animals we plan to eat, raising those animals,[13] processing the food, and moving it around the globe generates about a third of the heat-trapping gases that are released into the atmosphere.

We ask all living things on the planet to pay for that cost. Animals (like elephants and polar bears) risk extinction because they can't migrate to new habitats when their current water holes dry up or hunting grounds melt. People pay that cost as well, like islanders who become refugees as rising sea levels from melting ice caps flood their homeland and desert dwellers whose homes become drought-destroyed arid places.

I've wondered how it can be so much cheaper to import food than to buy local food. Again, the answer lies in invisible costs. Some costs are borne by field and factory laborers at home and especially abroad, and others by cows, hens, and sows kept in overcrowded and inhumane conditions so as to keep our milk, eggs, and bacon cheap.

We spend only 10 percent of our income on food because we don't pay our faraway and nearby neighbors who harvest our crops and butcher our beef a wage that covers their own food, shelter, and clothing. We also spend a smaller percentage of our income on food than we used to because gestating sows spend their lives in pens where they can only lie down on their chests (an unnatural position) or stand. A pregnant sow cannot even turn around. This intelligent sun-, mud-, and forest-loving animal (that can weigh up to nine hundred pounds) spends most of her life in a six-and-a-half-foot crate that is two feet wide with a slatted concrete floor that allows excrement to fall through. Before giving birth she is moved to a farrowing crate, which is slightly wider so that she can lie on her side to allow her babies (in a crate beside her) to reach through to nurse.[14] This is called "intensive pig farming," and it allows ranchers to turn a bigger profit than raising pigs in anything resembling their natural habitats or even something akin to Wilbur's pigpen in Uncle Homer's barn.

The public outcry concerning gestational crates has resulted in a ban in some states, similar to the banning of battery cages for laying hens. I'll talk about animals more in the next chapter, but learning the truth about these industries helps lift a veil that keeps us from seeing why our food is so cheap.

This is all very depressing. Is there any good news? If I buy fair-trade coffee to serve and pasture-raised pork, does that make any difference?

Yes, there is good news. And yes, it really does make a difference.

This spring Mark and I made the four-hour drive north for a speaking engagement at Seattle Pacific University. We went up a day early to enjoy Seattle, a break from tilling and planting before the onset of spring. At Pike's Place Market I bought a bottle of Indi's chocolate orange lotion, a favorite of mine since discovering it a year ago. Indi Chocolate is a small company whose owner sources chocolate directly from a farmers co-op. She pays better than fair-trade wages. Later we picked up our order of chocolate bars for the Fern Creek Market from Theo Chocolate and took a tour of Theo's plant, wanting to learn what we could about a company we'd be supporting.

We left inspired.

Theo (named after the theobroma cacao tree) also buys cocoa beans directly from farmers and ensures that workers are paid a fair wage and that they work in safe conditions in which no slave labor or trafficked children are used in the fields—where no synthetic pesticides, herbicides, or genetically modified seeds are used. Theo is committed to supporting farming practices that do not harm the earth, workers, or people who will eat the cocoa. So yes, people pay more for every bar of chocolate, but they are paying *a more accurate price* for what chocolate costs to make.

That makes them neighborly.

That good story can be retold with coffee, which can be sourced in similar ways, and with bananas, sugar, pineapple, mangoes, teas, and other foods grown only around the equator. Fair Trade Federation sets standards for wages, health and safety, and community investment and offers customers the assurance that they are supporting companies with integrity, which makes us good neighbors. Direct trade means coffee roasters and cacao bean buyers meet with farmers and farmer co-ops and arrange to buy from them directly, usually paying more than fair trade. Direct trade buyers prefer to know their farmers and the farming communities rather than to work through a third party.

Yes, there is potential for abusing the system—perhaps more so when it comes to the efforts of intensive farming operations that claim they are making the lives of chickens, pigs, and cows a little less miserable (does adding a few inches to a crate make life substantially better for a sow or a chicken?). If you have access to beef or pork or chicken or lamb from a source in your local neighborhood, you can go see where and how the animals live, and you can learn how they are raised and slaughtered.

If that's not possible (for most of us it's not), then I will trust a certifying body, imperfect as it may be, to be my witness concerning whether or not laborers are treated fairly and animals humanely. Besides, once I start being neighborly by considering the story behind chocolate or coffee, I'm inspired to look for other ways I can use my grocery dollars to be fair, just, and appreciative of the labor that others do so that I can enjoy the luxury of foods grown by neighbors near or far.

I planned to get some of my groceries at Walmart, but I keep hearing that Walmart has some unethical practices, and I suspect that you will say the same. But Walmart makes food less expensive for everyone, especially for people with low incomes, so why do they get so much bad press?

Here's my best effort at a short(ish) answer to a complex question. Although Walmart makes food and everything else it sells less expensive for consumers, it does so by passing on costs to taxpayers, to Walmart employees, to farm and factory workers abroad, to animals, and to the entire neighborhood—the ecosystems we all depend on. When understood from this perspective, it's not much of a savings for anyone.

Consider the people who work in places like Walmart (which is just one example, but a frequently cited one because they are our nation's largest corporate employer). While Walmart pays its employees at or slightly above minimum wage, Walmart has reduced the number of full-time employees it hires to avoid having to meet the requirements of the Affordable Health Care Act. However, Walmart does staff a full-time person who helps employees sign up for Medicaid and SNAP (Supplemental Nutritional Assistance Program)—government assistance programs for people who don't receive medical benefits from their jobs or whose income qualifies them for food stamps.[15] According to an article in *Forbes*, late in 2013 Walmart announced that they would transition a number of part-time jobs back to full-time—a decision that was motivated by the dramatic drop in sales that followed their decision to staff stores with temporary and part-time help.[16] I'd like to think the change was also motivated by a concern for employees, but in October of 2014, Walmart decided to eliminate health care benefits for its 30,000 employees working less than thirty hours a week. Under the Affordable Health Care Act, companies aren't required to provide health care to employees working fewer than thirty hours per week, and Walmart executives (like other large companies) are passing on the cost of their employees' medical care to taxpayers.[17]

Workers overseas also carry the cost of the cheaper prices we pay. Many products that fill the shelves are made in factories where laborers can be paid far less than minimum wage (generally something like a couple of dollars a day) and who work in conditions so unsafe that they wouldn't be tolerated in the United States.

Walmart can undersell whatever the local bakery, general store, or nursery is offering, so the typical pattern is to outcompete and close down the local competition. And while competition is supposed to work that way, maybe that sort of competition doesn't represent the highest virtue. When competition changes the character of a community by forcing out local family businesses that have neighborly connections and concerns, maybe the competitive edge should be questioned. When a multinational company takes over business, money that used to move around and stimulate the local economy is sent to Walmart headquarters and distributed to upper-level executives, Walton family members, and stockholders, undermining the economic stability of local communities.

So long as I'm offering up a critique of Walmart, a final reason it is often criticized is the repeated disregard it shows for the environment. In 2013, it was sued for $82 million for improperly dumping hazardous waste in California and Missouri. Ignacia S. Moreno, the assistant attorney general for the Justice Department's Environment and Natural Resources Division, said that Walmart "put the public and the environment at risk and gained an unfair economic advantage over other companies."[18] Walmart (and other offending corporations) pays its fines and continues business mostly as usual, sometimes offering a plan to improve. However, in the last ten years Walmart has been sued multiple times for breaking environmental laws, which suggests that the improvement plans aren't much of an improvement. In the last few years it has been sued for more than $110 million, but with an annual intake of $128 billion, a Walmart spokesperson said that the payments don't negatively affect their business.[19]

In contrast, food at Whole Foods is more expensive in part because employees earn, on average, fifteen dollars an hour and have a good benefit package, which the employees vote on every year. Still, Whole Foods is not above reproach. They, along with some cosmetic companies, were sued by the state of California in 2009 for deceptive labeling of cosmetics and household cleaners that tested positive for a carcinogenic that is required by law to be labeled in California. And while Whole Foods is mostly a transparent company, in 2014 it was hit with a lawsuit for unauthorized background screening of prospective employees in violation of the Fair Credit Reporting Act. Even "good and ethical" companies can find themselves on the other side of the law.

On the upside, Whole Foods company policy caps the CEO salary to not more than nineteen times what other employees earn (in terms of ratio, that's 19:1), which means Walter Robb, the current co-CEO, makes quite a bit less than other corporate CEOs.[20] As a comparison, the pay ratio for the CEO of Walmart to the average employee is 1,034:1.[21]

Whole Foods benefits include vacation time, education assistance, a good medical plan, and healthy-living incentives. For sixteen years it has been on *Fortune*'s list of "100 Best Companies to Work For." Food also costs more at places like Whole Foods (and similar markets) because they offer more fair-trade products, organic foods, sustainably and ethically grown foods, and eggs and meat from humanely raised animals. Shoppers are asked to pay a more accurate price for the real cost of food.

That being said, both Whole Foods and Walmart are big box stores. In neither case do they represent food that is primarily grown close to home.

Many of us have alternatives to buying our food from either Walmart or Whole Foods. By doing so, we are able to keep money in the community where it directly supports local farmers, ranchers, bakers, and other food, goods, and service providers, indirectly enriching the whole neighborhood.

The Alternative: From Farm to Fork

Every Monday and Thursday afternoon from the end of May through the beginning of November, Fern Creek Farm opens for pickup day. A dozen cars come, and anywhere from one to five people spill out and make their way to the market to fill wooden crates with whatever the fields offered up that week. All told, our CSA members take home food that feeds about one hundred people every week.

During the first weeks members choose between large heads of lettuce with names like Lovelock, Sylvesta, and Red Fire. They select between collards, rainbow chard, and a variety of kales kept fresh in large navy-blue canners speckled with white; they weigh out a pound or two of early red potatoes. Over the course of the season, members will weigh more potatoes and peas, beans, broccoli, and tomatoes on an antique scale that hangs in a corner of the market. We found it on eBay, and Mark and I bought it for each other for a Valentine's Day gift, an affirmation to each other that gifts of love don't have to include flowers and Hershey's chocolate.

At any rate, we don't start the season until the sun and soil have made the strawberries sweet and red, so each member picks up a couple of pint cartons, which we still call hallocks—a bygone term from the strawberry-picking days of our youth. Eggs from our hens, green onions, radishes, snow and snap peas, chives, and mint finish out those early crates, along with something extra, like a tomato or basil plant left over from planting and eager to get into some dirt.

By early July the food doesn't fit in the crate anymore. It hardly fits in our market. Summer and winter squash spill over their boxes, along with tomatoes, corn, broccoli, cabbage, carrots, beets, cucumbers, eggplant, peppers, onions, apples, peaches, oregano, basil, lavender, and thyme. The market fills with fragrances of summer and colors born in the sun.

Introverts that we are, we still manage to host an ice-cream social at the beginning of the season. Homemade ice cream, fresh strawberries, and toppings brought by our members grace the tables. People sit on blankets and chairs, toss beanbags, visit the hens, follow the paths through the forest, and play on the swing hanging under the giant maple tree.

Somewhere a sense of community takes root in the middle of eating ice cream, meeting new babies, feeding the hens wheat berries, and sitting on the saddle of the Giraffe Tree (picture a tree in the shape of a giraffe with a really long neck—a tree that should have died in whatever storm bent its trunk, but instead turned toward the sky and lived). We share a common place and common weather—cool rain in June and the dry heat of August. Our stories weave together through the shared histories of schools and churches attended, outdoor local concerts where we bump into each other, or the new bakery in town that a number of folks helped get off the ground. In some not-easily-understood way, we belong to each other and to this place, which can seem as intangible as belonging to God.

"We need to cultivate freedom, to cultivate hope, to cultivate diversity," Shiva told the Kansas City audience. "We need to build the direct relationship between those who grow the food and those who eat it. Care for people has to be the guiding force for how we produce, process, and distribute our food."[22] That's the hope and dream of the local food movement.

Fern Creek represents only one farm-to-fork alternative to buying produce grown God knows where by unknown others under unknown conditions. Local food alternatives edge forward, making agribusiness nervous enough to lobby for legislation that would limit what small farms and farmers can offer.

Cities across North America and Western Europe are doing again what the majority world never stopped doing—selling goods between neighbors. This primarily takes place at farmers markets, where fruits and vegetables, eggs and cheese, honey and maple syrup, meat and fish, flowers and crafts, Tibetan dumplings, and Indian satay are bought and sold. In rural communities, small towns, and large cities, people are gaining access to eggs from hens that feel rain and sunshine on their backs, honey from bees pollinating local fruit orchards and gardens, and meat and dairy from animals grown and raised in the county fields. Between vibrant farmers markets, community gardens, CSAs, and a renewed interest in local farm stands and U-Pick opportunities, most of us can get a fair amount of our food close to home.

Farmers and local communities are returning home from exile and finding ways to live peaceably, sustainably, and joyfully. These flourishing communities foster delight by eating in neighborly ways that acknowledge various memberships and obligations.

Of Bakeries, Cafés, Bookstores, and Other Local Establishments

This morning I'm writing at Newberg Bakery, which has been open nearly two months. The initial blush of infatuation has settled, and lines don't form outside the door so much anymore. It is possible to get a table and feel okay about staying awhile. Beside my computer sits a half-eaten marionberry-filled cinnamon roll and a cup of coffee. Both will be gone before I leave. Meanwhile, I'm working hard to concentrate on the gloom of the industrialized global food system as I sit in this light- and life-filled space.

Emily comes over to say hi and tells me she is enjoying getting to know my daughter Megan Anna as well as Kim on Monday nights. I'm feeling happy about that and imagining the ebb and flow of women in their early thirties talking about personal aspirations, motherhood, marriage, and being single.

I'm sure they don't talk about their mothers.

Jeff stops by to say hi too; he talks about Ed and Liz, our Fern Creek apprentices, who are good friends of his daughter. Who knew?

I wave and smile at Caitlin, one of our CSA members, and Brandon, the stay-at-home dad who loves to cook. John is grading at a corner table and nods as our eyes meet. Mark and I go to George Fox University plays and Newberg community plays with John and his wife, Cindy.

It seems like half the people I've talked about in this book meandered into the bakery this morning, either in person or in one conversation or another. People come and go; I recognize nearly half of them, which is not surprising since the people supporting this start-up bakery are people I run into at other local food gatherings.

A long beautiful table sits a bit to the side of the dining area—the community table, it's called. Mismatched plates, mugs, and silverware complement assorted chairs and tables. The walls are made of wood off an old barn, making it seem like I've walked into the eating space of a dear friend—a down-to-earth sort of friend likely to have flour on her cheeks, twinkly eyes, and a welcome smile. I feel at home here. This is my community, and it is simply lovely.

Brenda co-owns Newberg Bakery with Bruce. She's the pastry and cookie maker, and he's the bread baker. Brenda lets me in on a Monday a week later; they are closed to the public on Mondays, but it's certainly not a day "off."

Bruce and Brenda have dreamed about opening a bakery together for the last thirteen years, driven by a passion and desire to bake for their community. Prior to quitting her job to start the bakery, Brenda worked at George Fox University, where she regularly graced colleagues and students with scones she'd make at four thirty in the morning. She wanted students to find a place at school that felt like home, and Brenda and Bruce hold that hope for the bakery. They have created a community-minded space characterized by simplicity, both in ambiance and in the breads they bake.

Both of them left paying jobs with benefits for a local start-up business that pays little (they've yet to pay themselves) and requires them to work long hours on their feet, doing what most professionals would consider manual labor. "We choose it because it's a passion," she said, shrugging her shoulders. "For both of us. I can do it because my husband has a job with benefits. It's harder for Bruce. But we both, and Bruce especially, are content to live simply."

We talked about what would make it sustainable. Newberg Bakery is open Tuesday through Saturday, from 6:00 a.m. to 4:00 p.m. Brenda and Bruce arrive by four o'clock in the morning and don't get home until six thirty or seven o'clock in the evening. They have three employees but will need to hire more to make this life sustainable, no matter how much passion they have for it.

I asked her how they would know whether they have succeeded, and Brenda said, "We're successful already, depending on how you define it, because Newberg has embraced us so fully, so incredibly." Her only disappointment seems to be disappointing people. In the hour we talked, four clusters of people tried the door and found it locked. Brenda avoided eye contact with them, waiting for them to go away. The first few weeks they were open from 6:00 a.m. to 6:00 p.m. and weren't getting home before ten o'clock at night; now that they close at four, she feels like she is disappointing people, but we agreed that the new hours help make the endeavor sustainable.

For the local food movement to work, we will have to accept limits, like not expecting tomatoes in February and fresh bread whenever we want it. We'll have to plan ahead, as our grandparents did, and get our bread for Sunday on Saturday; we will need to can tomatoes in September if we want them in February. The variety and convenience of our food will diminish to an extent, but the quality will be better. In the case of Newberg residents looking for baked goods, it will be literally infused with grace. As a Quaker, Brenda infuses her baking with prayer.

> When I bake I pray for people. That is a huge part of bread baking for me. I will probably get teary as I say this, but every morning when I baked for students I would pray my scone prayer over them and weep. I've trained myself not to weep here; but the early morning hours are quiet, and I still pray my scone prayer and pray for the people that will come through our doors that day. I pray that they will sense God and that they will know this place is safe and find it a comforting place, a community space that they can call home.[23]

Brenda captures my hope for the local food movement. Motivated by affection, by a passion to create and to nourish those in her community, she welcomes people into her space and treats them with kindness and warmth. For this to be sustainable, she and Bruce will have to figure out how to take time off. Maybe we will have to be willing to pay more for our bread so they can hire more help. It will require us as their community to recognize that they close on Sundays and Mondays—even though they know it is bad for business and disappointing to customers—because it is essential for their well-being. It is in our interest for this to be a sustainable enterprise. Already they've talked about closing for a week now and then. Bruce has an out-of-the-country wedding to attend in a few months, and they both will need time off to rest, to go places they can't otherwise visit. Meanwhile, we will be given a chance to remember what Newberg was like before we had a bakery; hopefully, their absence will cause us to be extra thankful.

✤ *Brenda's Scone Prayer* ✤

Jesus, your creative presence inspires me to create by baking.

As I gather my ingredients, gather people close to your heart. With flour, sugar, baking powder, and salt being blended together, cause us to become inseparable from you, as we are nothing on our own.

As the butter is cut into the flour, please bring richness to our lives. Cause each person to be a delight to you and to each other.

As I add these chocolate chips, guide our footsteps that we will not stumble over things in our path nor cause others to stumble and fall.

As the milk is poured in, pour your fullness into us. Soften our hearts to hear you. Bind us together as your followers and as community. As the flour becomes dough, shape us and mold us after you. Cause us to be all that you have created us to be.

With the egg wash brushed over the top, cover us with your love, grace, and mercy.

May the heat of the oven transform us and make us new. May each of us know your love and filling presence. Satisfy the inward longings and desires that you've placed within us.

We are your new creation and you delight in us. Cause us to be a delight to you.

Aggressive Lovingkindness

The local food movement is a global one, and I'm in good company when I claim that it can heal a planet in trouble. The movement is an aggressive form of lovingkindness that lessens the negative impact of conventional agricultural practices and relies on a guiding principle of neighborliness over profit. The movement will thrive or fail based on the links forged between local food providers and their communities. Farmers, bakers, ranchers, and dairies are ready to provide the alternative but depend on people willing to support their efforts by paying something closer to the real cost of food. Such support requires aggressive lovingkindness—a desire to pursue justice, integrity, good stewardship, and sacrifice. Below are four practices for making a beginning.

First, experiment with eating more locally and seasonally. This is a straightforward way to be neighborly—both directly to local farmers and indirectly to distant neighbors sharing the planet. Buy bread from a local bakery and eggs, if you can, from a neighbor or a local farmer. Choose one item that you buy regularly and decide to buy it locally and seasonally—perhaps apples or broccoli or bread. Once that seems easy, add another item, building new habits gradually, step by step and choice by choice. Enjoy strawberries in June, and then make jam and freeze the extra for strawberry smoothies in September and strawberry dumplings in January. *Simply in Season* by Mary Beth Lind and Cathleen Hockman-Wert and *From Asparagus to Zucchini* by the FairShare CSA Coalition are two of many cookbooks that help people figure out how to prepare vegetables like bok choy, fennel, and kohlrabi—new, old foods showing up at farmers markets and CSAs.

Second, for luxury items that require land and people near the equator to grow them, make the choice to buy fair trade and direct trade or to go without—or at least go with less. If you choose to enjoy the luxury of chocolate, coffee, and bananas, begin with one and decide to buy only fair or direct trade, to pay a price that better reflects what it costs the land and the people who grow and harvest it. Once you've succeeded with one of these choices, take another step. Practice aggressive lovingkindness.

I fail to practice this consistently. I still drink mochas—and not always from places that only source fair-trade coffee and chocolate. But I'm working on it, and bit by bit I'm building habits that will eventually become the only imaginable option. We try to make it easier for our CSA members by carrying organic and fair-trade baking cocoa and chocolate bars in the Fern Creek Market, as well as organic local butter from pasture-based cows. Changing a pattern starts with taking an initial step in a different direction.

Third, avoid food tainted with animal misery. I'll talk about this more in the next chapter, but consider how aggressive lovingkindness can extend to the hens that lay our eggs, the pigs that supply us with ham and bacon and sausage, and the cows whose newborn babies are taken from them year after year so that we can have milk, butter, and cheese. What does it look like to have compassion and affection for creatures on which we have come to depend?

Finally, experiment with eating lower on the food chain, which means meals without animal protein. Go meatless on Mondays. Then add to those meatless days as your repertoire of options and desire for variety grows. *More-with-Less*, a Mennonite cookbook by Doris Longacre, came out in response to the 1970s global food crisis, encouraging people to eat less meat or eat lower on the food chain to lessen our demand for food sourced from around an increasingly hungry world. Since then, plant-based diets have gained popularity. *The China Study: The Most Comprehensive Study of Nutrition Ever Conducted and the Startling Implications for Diet, Weight Loss, and Long-term Health* by Thomas Campbell and T. Colin Campbell looks at eating from a personal-health perspective, exploring the link between eating animal proteins and an assortment of chronic illnesses including heart disease, diabetes, and certain cancers. *The China Study* came out in 2005 and by 2013 had sold more than a million copies, making it one of the best-selling nutrition books in the United States. The authors—one a professor of nutritional biochemistry and the other a physician—based the book on a twenty-year study, and enough people have been compelled by their findings that plant-based or vegan cookbooks have shifted from the fringe to mainstream.

My favorite vegan cookbook is a twice-loved duct-taped copy of *Vegan Planet* by Robin Robertson. My daughter Sarah gave me her old copy after she received the newly revised edition to review on her blog, *My Darling Vegan*.[24] Teff and quinoa, tofu and tempeh, black beans and sweet potatoes, almonds and peanuts, and kale and mushrooms are just a few of the good-for-you foods that have prominent places in the pages of this hefty cookbook. Eating without meat is compassionate and opens the door to a world of delicious alternatives that are good for our bodies, our neighbors, and our planet.

A Final Word

We ask for feedback from our Fern Creek members every year. One question on our anonymous survey asks why they joined a CSA, since they could more easily go to the grocery store for their produce and have more freedom to select what they want. The following statements are some of their responses:

> We really enjoyed coming to the farm every week and being able to see where the food was grown and getting to know our farmers and their farming philosophies. The kids *loved* feeding the chickens and exploring the woods.

I appreciate the personal touch and consistency, and the variety that I wouldn't likely choose on my own. I also like the recipe suggestions!

We wanted to try the CSA since we eat local organic produce, and this was a good value. We felt that it would be good for the boys to see how food is grown as we work hard to educate them on healthy eating.

I like the relationship developed with the food and the farmer.

This captures the heart of the local food movement. Frances Lappé is best known for her book *A Diet for a Small Planet*, which came out in the early 1970s. Since then she has founded three national organizations that consider hunger, poverty, and the environmental crises as well as solutions to these problems. In an article she wrote for *The Nation*, she argues that global hunger is about having access to abundance rather than a lack of food. Of the local food movement she says:

> This rising global food movement taps universal human sensibilities—expressed in Hindu farmers in India saving seeds, Muslim farmers in Niger turning back the desert and Christian farmers in the United States practicing biblically in-spired Creation Care. In these movements lies the revolutionary power of the food movement: its capacity to upend a life-destroying belief system that has brought us power-concentrating corporatism. . . .
>
> At its best, this movement encourages us to "think like an ecosystem," en-abling us to see a place for ourselves connected to all others, for in ecological systems "there are no parts, only participants," German physicist Hans Peter Duerr reminds us. . . . As the food movement stirs, as well as meets, deep human needs for connection, power, and fairness, let's shed any notion that it's simply "nice" and seize its potential to break the spell of our disempowerment.[25]

Last week I visited my friend Allison in Tennessee. Wendell Berry was in Nashville, talking about what makes a healthy community, and Allison and I went to hear him. A lot of Berry's words struck a chord, given what I've been writing and thinking about recently. He said that conviviality, or neighborliness, brings healing to communities and that we had to get beyond *wishing* our neighbors well and actually *doing* something neighborly for them. Conviviality can be brought to distant neighbors too, he said, by holding ourselves to account when we use products that we don't know enough about to have a full accounting for what they cost.

Berry brought a grounded practicality to lofty ideas of community.

About a week after walking up my new neighbors' driveway, we found a note from them in our mailbox. Patsy wrote, "We are so sorry we missed you Sunday and wanted to thank you for the veggies. Your kindness is very much appreciated and we look forward to meeting you both in person. We've been in Oregon a very short time, and are glad to know we have some great neighbors."

I'm not, in fact, a great neighbor, not even a good one if I'm honest with how often I stumble to get beyond well-wishing. But I'm taking steps toward being a better neighbor to those both near and far.

• Brenda Burg's Scones with Love and Prayers •

2 c.	flour
3 tbsp.	sugar
2 tsp.	baking powder
½ tsp.	salt
6 tbsp.	unsalted butter (if you use salted butter, cut salt to ¼ tsp.)
½ c.	milk (more as needed, a little at a time)
1 egg	beaten thoroughly, to brush on top of scones

Preheat oven to 425 degrees. Mix dry ingredients together. Cut in butter. Add chocolate chips, nuts, and/or dried fruit if desired (see variations below). Stir in milk. Dough should be fairly dry, not sticky. Place on lightly floured counter and pat into an 8-inch circle about ½ to ⅝ inches. Cut into 8–10 equal parts (or make smaller scones by cutting the dough in half and patting each half into a 6- to 7-inch circle, cutting each into 8–10 equal parts). Place on a cookie sheet lined with parchment paper (ideal, but not necessary). Brush egg on the top and sides of each scone. Bake for 15–18 minutes and cool on wire racks.

Variations: Starter Ideas

Cranberry / Orange Cornmeal

Substitute 1 cup corn meal for 1 cup flour; add 1 cup cranberries (fresh, dried, or frozen—baker's choice). Use ¼ cup orange juice, ¼ cup milk, and add orange zest to taste.

Oatmeal / Raisin (or Date)

Substitute 1 cup crushed oatmeal for 1 cup flour (place dry ingredients in a food processor, add the butter and pulse until sand-like); add ¾ to 1 cup raisins or chopped dates just before the milk. Add chopped nuts (optional).

Lemon Poppy Seed

Add 2 tablespoons poppy seeds; use ¼ cup lemon juice with ¼ cup milk, and add lemon zest. Omit egg on top. After baking, brush on a mixture of 1 cup powdered sugar, 1–2 tablespoons lemon juice, and lemon zest.

Reflections and Questions

1. Can you name the neighbors who live closest to you? What do you know about them? Have you ever helped each other out? In general, how do you feel about your neighbors' sense of neighborliness? How about your own sense of neighborliness toward them?

2. Do you see neighborliness as nice, but optional? Reflect on how it feels to consider neighborliness as an expression of your faith rather than "nice, but optional."

3. In what ways does embracing a global neighborhood seem overwhelming? To make any challenge manageable it's helpful to take one step at a time. What one step could you take toward being a better global neighbor? Do you have a small group or some friends with whom you could talk about this and take a step together?

4. After reading the chapter, what sticks with you more, the hopeless picture of industrialized food or the hopeful resurgence of local and just food? Why do you think you gravitate toward either hopelessness or hopefulness? Either way, what would it take to strengthen hopefulness?

5. Think about how you already participate in the resurgence of local and just food. Then think about what next step you could take toward supporting local and just food.

6. Do you have a farmers market in your area? If yes, do you shop there? What motivates you, and what do you find satisfying about it? If you've never been or if you went once and haven't been back, what keeps you away?

7. The chapter offers four practices that move us toward local and just eating. Consider choosing one practice to experiment with this week. Afterward, reflect on how it felt to be intentional in regard to food and how being neighborly is affecting how you see God, your place in the world, and your relationship with God.

5

Harvesting

Labors of Love

How calmly,
as though it were an ordinary thing,
we eat the blessed earth.

—Mary Oliver,
from "Beans Green and Yellow"[1]

We start at eight o'clock in the morning, gathering with our apprentices for a devotional reflection to set the day. Then we head to the Hazelnut Patch (I have a penchant for naming things—like the beds surrounded by hazelnut shells that we spread to discourage slugs) to harvest various greens and fennel, and we collect the berries before they, or we, grow overly warm. From the Trellis Garden we'll gather snow and snap peas and, later in the season, pole beans and tomatoes. From the main fields we'll dig potatoes and bring in corn, beets, carrots, eggplant, squash, and cucumbers.

We welcome the morning before the Oregon sun—temperate though it may be—has a chance to exact too much from us or the fruits and vegetables that we will harvest. I find it oddly comforting when I am feeling a bit scorched and wilted to remember that we depend on that hot star to make food grow.

The harvest season begins as soon as the strawberries are ready and ends before Thanksgiving—after the abundance of tomatoes and zucchini have exhausted themselves, after harvest days have turned rainy and colder. In those latter days we mostly distribute food that's already been harvested: butternut and baby blue Hubbard squash, Yukon Gold and Russet potatoes, and Cortland storage onions. But still, in early November we'll go to the field to harvest kale and broccoli, which give all season long, and leeks, parsnips, and late cabbage.

Food is evidence of God's grace. Variety is evidence of God's creativity and abundance of God's generosity.

Jesus called forth abundance from the Sea of Galilee into the nets of Peter, James, and John—so much abundance that they needed help to bring it in. So much that it tore their nets and threatened to sink their boats. Jesus told his disciples, "The harvest is great, but the workers are few. So pray to the Lord who is in charge of the harvest; ask him to send more workers into his fields" (Luke 10:2). The harvest metaphor works for the good news of the gospel because people of that day understood what it meant to have abundance without enough hands to bring it in. Just about everybody appreciates abundance.

A plentiful harvest requires a good bit of labor, and considering the various animals we eat, milk we drink, and eggs and honey we consume, harvesting also requires sacrifice. Abundance and sacrifice constitute two ingredients of a good harvest.

The truth of the matter is, we grow plants and animals up strong so that we can sacrifice them in order to live. Instead of relishing only the mouthwatering abundance of the harvest, can we also hold in our mind's eye the labor and sacrifice that are required for us to eat well? Might looking at food labor and sacrifice incline us to become humbly grateful in a way that draws us toward food raised and harvested in affectionate—that is, ethical—ways? How would it change our perception of food to remember that we cannot live unless someone works to bring food in from the field and that living things are required to give up what they cherish (calves and mamas in the case of dairy farming, a hen's eggs, the bees' honey, and the animals' very lives) so that we can be nourished by their bodies?

I didn't become grateful for the labor of farmhands and the sacrifice of dairy cows and honey bees until I became a farmer. For years I ate with no awareness of the work and sacrifices of others. Awakening to gratitude brought a hunger for *just* food: food gathered using harvesting practices that are defined by good husbandry—practices that mirror the Good Shepherd—and good farming that mirrors the Creator who walked with Adam and Eve and taught them how to take care of Eden.

But on this first harvest day of our sixth season as CSA (community supported agriculture) farmers, I am thinking mostly of abundance as we cut heads of bok choy and pull up heads of smooth, green lettuce (tinged with red) and pick red, sun-sweetened berries one by one. Turns out the closer I am to the actual harvest, the more aware I am of abundance, the more mindful I am of the various kinds of work and sacrifice required to bring it in, and the more likely I am to feel affection for the land, plants, and living beings, including the people who help to provide my sustenance.

Abundance

I can be stingy or generous, and while my inclination leans more often toward stingy (which I prefer to call *resourceful frugality*), a surprising love fills my throat and heart when I throw myself toward generosity. I hope it is unexpected gratitude taking up residence.

Liz and Kara, last year's summer apprentices, wanted to bake cookies to put out for our CSA members as they picked up their crates. When Liz told me, I was caught off guard by the fullness in my throat; I was nearly overcome by the ordinary idea of simple hospitality. Maybe it's because one year I tried to *sell* cookies to CSA members (for the most part they remained unsold, and our summer apprentices, Mark, and I ate them). The idea of *giving* them away struck me as so very right in that moment. It's a no-strings-attached gift to subscribers who support our micro-farming endeavor. Liz and Kara inspired me, as youthful optimism is wont to do. "Yes, we could take turns baking things," I said, not wanting to be left out of the gifting. Why not bake up lavender shortbread, peanut butter cookies, and zucchini bread to give away?

Why not throw ourselves toward abundant generosity and see what comes? I long to live a life defined by the generosity that recognizes abundance and bespeaks a heart awakened by gratitude. Resourceful frugality has a place, though perhaps I should apply it more often to what I consume rather than what I might give away.

The abundance of God's creation reaches well beyond food. To stand on the Pacific shore—feet washed by salty water that has traveled a great distance—is to stand on the edge of a vastness in which living things stir and teem, play and hunt; it is hardly imaginable. Abundance resides in the magnificence of Colorado's snow-peaked mountains, the expanse of a great prairie, or even in the tiny wonders that inhabit a small prairie or pond. Each is a compass pointing toward God, the giver of life and all things.

I see abundance in the thousands of bees that leave when one of Fern Creek's colonies splits to send a contingency forth to start a new hive elsewhere. For a few days bees cluster in a large oval-shaped ball, clinging to some branch nearby while scouts go out to find a suitable home. And then, to stand beneath the swarm as it takes to the sky, skimming along about twenty feet above the ground on their way to their new home! O the abundance of life swarming just overhead!

Abundance shows up in the love that friends and family give to each other, even when they can't afford the time, and in the volunteer hours people give to strangers through organizations like Love INC (Love In the Name of Christ), which provides an assortment of services to the underserved and disenfranchised in our communities. Abundant love comes from adults who care for babies in nurseries and teach children in Sunday schools around the world, and in the general commitment to neighborliness that is expressed in thousands of ways.

God is in the midst of that abundance.

I value abundance more when I know something of the sacrifice required to bring it about. Sometimes, but not always, I manage to keep my eyes open once a thing creeps into my vision. I want to be as open-eyed about sacrifices related to food as I am when a black and yellow garden spider (known in more heady circles as the *argiope aurantia*) moves toward me on a gossamer thread from her web in the center of a Cherokee Purple tomato plant. I become quite mindful of my eight-legged neighbor, who eats aphids and has come to watch me harvest. I try not to lose sight of this yellow and black, scary-looking friend once I've seen her. I've come to learn that scary things right in front of me are easier to stay mindful of than scary things far away. As uncomfortable as it is, part of what I hope to do in this chapter is to bring some of those scary things closer to home, to expose hidden food-harvesting practices that bring avoidable and unnecessary suffering to people and animals.

I prefer to see this task as an invitation to mindfulness, which helps us enjoy the abundance surrounding us. Might paying attention incline us to partake in abundance with hearts full of love—that is, with cleaner hands and clearer consciences? Once I opened the door of mindfulness, a mostly welcome discomfort wafted into our home. I want to believe that I live with integrity and compassion and am humbled when I see ways that I fail, ways that I put myself before all else. Sometimes I choose to turn away and "forget" what I know because, well, I suppose sometimes I just want what I want. I am not proud of this and do not find my "forgetting" particularly excusable.

It only comforts me a little to know that I am not alone in this.

It's easy for people in the post-industrialized world to not be mindful of the work and sacrifice that go into the growing, planting, and harvesting of food because we've become used to accepting the abundance without question. I sometimes feel as though the people who question how our food system works are perceived as being unappreciative or lacking in gratitude for the very good lives we have access to in Western Europe and North America.

But I'll take the risk and forge ahead because bad things happen in the food business, and I choose to believe that responsible consumers—people whose lives are characterized by compassion and love—would want to know. Besides, it's easier not to be informed because most food work happens far away from us. For the most part, it is invisible work that takes place behind concrete walls. In vague terms, we assume that machines harvest more crops than people do, so we don't know when and how people are involved in the harvesting process. We know animals are raised for food, and frankly, a lot of us find our ignorance of that process a comfort. I didn't really want to know how chicks, piglets, calves, and lambs got from their newborn state to plastic-wrapped packages of breasts, bacon, hamburger, or lamb shank in the grocery store. We don't know because food is harvested differently than it was a century or even a lifetime ago.

From Small-Scale to Large-Scale Harvesting

You've likely noticed that most agricultural history lessons start with the Industrial Revolution. So much social, religious, and agricultural life changed with the advent of mechanized industry.

Nearly two hundred years ago, the West experienced the beginning of what became a massive migration of people leaving rural communities for potential jobs in the teeming cities. Inventions of the Industrial Revolution replaced human labor with machines. The combine, for instance, combined harvesting, gathering, and threshing into one task that could be done by one person driving a machine (air-conditioned cabs showed up in the 1970s) over ripened fields. If sons and daughters wanted to escape the farm for jobs in the city, the combine made it possible. Fewer laborers were needed on the farm, and sons and daughters could set out to seek their fortunes.

And that's how people came to think of it. City life, or at least life *off* the farm, would be the better life, the easier life, the life with a secure income.

The Industrial Revolution made it possible for people with an education to stop doing unskilled physical labor and to work with their minds instead—as though farming requires neither intelligence nor skill. Collectively, we decided that we needed more teachers, doctors, designers, therapists, and event planners. Helping children to get an education so that they could leave the farm came to be seen as the better choice, the choice that would give them happier lives.

Even for those who didn't see the farm as a place they needed to escape and who valued their relationship to and connection with land, the combine and other tractor implements made a lot of farm labor obsolete. Farming became efficient, and food could be sold for less. Family farms that tried to farm with traditional methods couldn't compete. They couldn't sell their crops for enough to cover their expenses and ended up selling their farms to those who could farm thousands of acres with machines. Even though they wanted to stay, a number of farming families were forced to migrate to cities for jobs.

That same migration has been under way in the Global South since the mid-twentieth century. About half of the world's population now lives in urban areas, with the most rapid migration from rural to urban communities currently happening in Africa and Asia.[2] Over the last fifty years, many of these people have lost control of land their families had farmed (without owning) for thousands of years. In their minds, it is the land of their ancestors—a communal land they belong to rather than own. As land they've lived on gets sold or leased to multinational corporations for agricultural use, some stay and work on the new plantations, receiving less-than-subsistence pay to do the agricultural work that has not been mechanized. The rest become land refugees and relocate to the city in hopes of finding low-skilled work, since there is no place for them to practice and live using their remarkable skills in subsistence farming.

Historically, migration is most often connected to economics, to the pull of opportunity elsewhere when opportunity at home disappears. This happens both between countries and also within them and is primarily experienced as a move from rural areas to urban ones. Migration also occurs involuntarily—through people-trafficking and slavery and fleeing ethnic cleansing or other forms of freedom- and life-threatening oppression. The wave of migration currently under way is also complicated by changing climates. Environmental refugees are on the move as long-term droughts expand deserts and make homelands unlivable, as wet climates relentlessly flood, and as coastal land permanently disappears under rising sea levels. Farmers and ranchers in the United States are also experiencing some of the effects of climate change. The drought that began in 2010 continues to affect places throughout North America, hitting Texas and California the hardest. Similarly, we've experienced more floods and hurricanes in recent years, which have wreaked havoc on coastal cities—particularly those at sea level. In the United States we generally have access to insurance and government aid to help ease the economic losses. The Global South has fewer resources to help them recover from weather-related disasters. In 2013, the world experienced forty-one disasters that cost a billion dollars or more each, which is the largest number on record, according to the Annual Global Climate and Catastrophe Report.[3] For all of these reasons, living off the land, particularly for farmers and ranchers in the Global South, has become increasingly difficult.

Furthermore, expanding global trade became a hoped-for pathway to world peace after WWII. While some progress toward harmony probably occurred, the more obvious result was that trade reforms opened doors for multinational corporations to expand into new places, where they took control of crops like bananas, cocoa, sugar, and (more recently) quinoa from South America and teff from Ethiopia.

On the upside, agricultural inventions gave people freedom to do something besides farm and made food less expensive to produce and cheaper to buy. On the downside, we lost our connection to one of the most fundamental of human activities: the growing and harvesting of food. We lost our sense of where abundance comes from, our ability to know the costs and labor required, and connections that would incline us toward affection for land, animals, ranchers, and farmers.

A Mindful Harvest

In our last batch of chicks we discovered two roosters. The discovery happens around adolescence, when their feathers begin to outshine those of their female counterparts, and they start to practice crowing.

Thing is, we don't keep roosters.

Mark would say we don't keep them on account of neighborliness, and that's true enough. Roosters welcome the coming day with enthusiasm, and when daybreak comes at four thirty, that's a mighty early wake-up call.

I tried selling these beautiful auburn- and rust-feathered roosters on Craigslist and on our Fern Creek Facebook page. Failing that, I tried giving them away. But as no one was in the market for a couple of young Rhode Island Reds, we ended up slaughtering them. "Noooooooo!" my niece responded in a Facebook reply, expressing appropriate grief. Indeed, this is the hardest task we undertake as stewards of Fern Creek. We struggle with the power we have to determine what lives and what dies, especially when being neighborly to one sort of neighbor requires us to sacrifice another. Mark does the killing, and I do the de-feathering and cleaning; while my task takes longer and is messier, I prefer it.

This is how it goes down. Generally, I go and get the rooster because I am shorter and move slower (oddly an advantage here), making me less intimidating than Mark. After cornering and catching the rooster, I carry it to Mark, who is waiting by the Killing Tree. Mark made a cone-shaped box he nailed to a tree so that he can put the rooster in upside down. The contraption snuggly holds the rooster with his head sticking through the bottom; chickens go to a quiet place when they are held upside down. It may be because they are helpless or because their blood rushes to their head, but it makes for a calm killing—one that feels humane—though it's hard to know for sure.

On the way to the Killing Tree, I thank the rooster for his life and for the sustenance we will get from his death. I apologize and express my hope that he has enjoyed life at Fern Creek. Once I hand him off to Mark I leave, and Mark brings the rooster back to me after his headless body has stopped jerking.

Knowing we had two roosters to "process" (a euphemism used by those who would call our Killing Tree the "Processing Tree" to soften the edges), I asked Liz if she wanted to participate. Liz is a nursing student, and I figured the cleaning process might be interesting to her. Even so, I expected her to say no. She said yes, and her yes meant she wanted to participate in the entire process. She stood with Mark and watched the roosters die, and then she and I each de-feathered and cleaned a bird. We finished the task by cooking each of the animals in our own way. The meat was tender but also tasted earthy, perhaps because it came from a young rooster that had been running around and crowing at the world a couple of days earlier.

Sometimes I find it necessary to repeat this truth to myself: sacrifice is part of the abundance that allows us to live. Not that people have to eat animals to live. We are omnivores and can get all the nutrients we need from plants. But some animals (cats and hawks, for instance) are carnivores, and other animals must die for them to live. Make no mistake, the food chain is as violent as it is functional.

Until we learned that catch and release is illegal in Oregon, we captured, relocated, and released squirrels feasting in the garden. If squirrel were a part of our diet, I suppose I would feel better about killing them, grateful for an easily harvested form of sustenance—and pest control besides. But we're a generation or two removed from eating squirrel, so we remain conflicted about this seemingly unnecessary sacrifice of life, although in the case of mice and gophers we can kill with less angst.

Philosophers and social scientists draw a distinction between profane violence (senseless, with no purpose or good end) and sacred violence (which serves some unifying purpose or greater good). Drunken brawls are a form of profane violence. Fighting to overthrow a tyrant who oppresses you, your family, and your people might be regarded as sacred violence. James Craig Anderson, a forty-nine-year-old African American, was on his way home from work when he was beaten and then run over by a group of teenagers who said that they were on the hunt for someone black and that they chose Anderson randomly. That 2011 tragedy epitomizes profane violence and is indicative of the racial hatred still present in the United States. While the killing of Jesus was equally profane in many ways, it is a violence that most Christians accept as necessary and explain in theological terms. In purely sociological terms, Jesus's crucifixion is perceived as "sacred" both because of the significance given to it by Christians and because it served a greater purpose: the mobilization of a world religion.

If the difference between sacred and profane violence matters, then might it be relevant to think about the kinds of violence required in the harvesting of our food? To be mindful is to know enough about the process to be both humbled by and grateful for the work and cost of the harvest, acknowledging that violence is part of harvesting, which is part of eating.

Sitting with Violence

Good farming and good animal husbandry require compassion, attention, and love for place and the living things in that place. They also require sacrifice. Does it sound surprising to say that the closer one is to the harvest—to the reaping of both plants and animals—the more mindful one is of the true costs of food?

Norman Wirzba writes: "Eating is the daily reminder of creaturely mortality. We eat to live, knowing that without food we will starve and die. But to eat we must also kill, realizing that without the deaths of others—microbes, insects, plants, animals—we can have no food."[4]

Wirzba dedicates a chapter in *Food and Faith* to understanding the significance of sacrifice and a more redemptive view of death. Through a good death life moves forward. We are dependent on the death of plants and animals because we must consume them to live. The need for some measure of violence became more apparent to me once I started killing the occasional chicken or the cucumber beetles that devour our young squash plants.

Perhaps sacrifice, as understood in an agrarian society like ancient Israel, is a way to see the difference between the violence of animal slaughter that occurred on altars and in households and the violences that occur in slaughterhouses.

Sacrifice in Israel involved giving away a precious possession, released as a gift for another to sustain another life. The story of the Good Shepherd held more richness for a community that understood what being a good shepherd demanded. Animals received tender care, food, and water even at the discomfort and risk of the shepherd. A good shepherd took on the lion or bear or wolf, even at risk to his or her own life. Caring for these animals required a commitment to go seek for the one that was lost. When these cared-for creatures were presented to God as sacrifices, both the giver and the gift, according to Wirzba, were made sacred on account of that relationship.

The giving up, or sacrifice, of an animal for food was costly both to the animal (who had no say in the matter) and to the one who tended that animal with compassionate care. While the depth of that ritual is lost on us, it still offers an alternative to mass and impersonal killings that happen in slaughterhouses. Animal husbandry ends where the industrialized raising of animals begins. Slaughterhouses impose an impersonal violence, a profane violence that happens far away from our lamb-, beef-, chicken-, or pork-laden tables.

Profane Violence: The Dark Side of Harvesting

While any number of foods that we harvest would work as examples of the dark side of harvesting, I'll discuss two that I've already alluded to: cocoa fields in Africa and slaughterhouses in the United States. Both harvesting practices happen far enough away that it requires some work to learn about them. To become mindful—to eat with both gratitude and affection—harvesting practices like these need to become visible.

Cocoa Fields

Mark and I like chocolate. We drink it, eat 70 and 85 percent dark chocolate bars, and toss cocoa powder or chocolate chips into cookie batter, pudding cakes, breads, and brownies. We stock baking and drinking cocoa, salted almond and coconut dark chocolate bars, and bittersweet chocolate chips in the Fern Creek Market—dedicating a whole shelf to a food that only grows near the equator. Like coffee and bananas, we depend on people primarily from West African and Central American countries to grow cocoa beans for us. The chocolate in the Fern Creek Market is grown and harvested by farmers and farming communities paid a fair wage for their labor.

That makes this chocolate cost more. Those who purchase it are bearing the real cost of growing, harvesting, and processing cocoa. It requires commitment to purchase it when cheaper alternatives are easily available. Fair trade and direct trade ensure that the people who work to supply both raw and value-added products like sugar, coffee, chocolate, bananas, and clothes are paid a fair wage—that is, a livable wage—and that they work in relatively safe conditions (at least compared to non-fair-trade factories and plantations). All of us would like to assume that multinational corporations are concerned for the well-being of their workers, that they invest in the lives of the people providing the labor that brings in profit. We don't want to believe that corporations move factories from country to country, following the dictators or governing officials that promise them the cheapest labor and the least amount of regulation.

But ethics in the workplace brings down profits, at least when profitability is measured in dollars. Enough people are becoming aware of the dark side of chocolate to demand greater accountability for multinational giants like Nestle and Hershey. To be clear, it's not that Nestle goes out and tells cocoa farmers to kidnap children to work in the fields; they simply buy from the buyer who can bring them the best price. That's sound economics.

Not all Nestle, Hershey, or Godiva workers are trafficked children. Some children are sent to work in cocoa fields by parents so they can feed their other children or perhaps send one or two children to school, which is free so long as you can afford the uniforms and books. Many cocoa workers are adults, who are paid pennies for their labor—so few, in fact, that the whole family must work to afford the grain that will keep them alive. They could never afford a Milky Way and would be appalled at the price of one.

That we use chocolate as a love language—some of our chocolate is even marketed as "Kisses"—requires a pretty specific focus of that chocolaty embrace. I'm rather fond of Mark's perspective that, while fair-trade chocolate chips cost anywhere from eight to twelve dollars a pound, we should be extravagant with our love and cook with them often. Eat chocolate chips on ice cream! Add them to chocolate zucchini cake! Make double chocolate cookies and give them away!

I've seen students become passionate about fair-trade chocolate, sugar, bananas, and coffee, and they have far less discretionary money than I do. After buying fair-trade bananas and chocolate for several months, I had a student tell me it's second nature now and that she chooses to go without chocolate when she can't afford it. Her commitment humbles me because her mindfulness has become an affection for people who work with foods grown near the equator, which makes purchasing any product that is not fair trade unthinkable. The more mindful one becomes, the easier it is for food choices to flow from affection, which is a better motivator for change than guilt.

My student's commitment is humbling for another reason: I recently purchased regular, non-fair-trade sugar to feed our bees (we go through a fair bit of it every year). At this point, I buy fair-trade sugar to cook with in my kitchen and non-fair-trade to make syrup for our bees in the spring and fall. I'm not sure how I justify this, but so far I have managed to do so. Every year.

Finding Fair-Trade Chocolate

Chocolate bars. Divine Chocolate is an African-owned farmers co-op that can export a finished product (e.g., chocolate bars) to the United States. It can be found in many grocery stores or ordered online. Explore their company philosophy and story, and place orders at divinechocolate.com.

Theo bars. For a more creative blending of flavors, go to Theo. Theo bars are distributed widely, and the company goes beyond fair trade, ensuring that workers at every step of the process are paid well and work in safe conditions. Explore and order online at theochocolate.com.

Cocoa powder. Everything that Mama Ganache Artisan Chocolate carries is fair trade and organic, which includes an assortment of bulk chocolate products like chocolate chips, drinking cocoa, and baking bars. Find them at mama-ganache.com.

In addition, Global Exchange is a nonprofit organization that works as a clearinghouse, selling a number of products grown and made around the world, including food items, clothing, jewelry, baskets, linens, pottery, and various household and yard art. Look them up at globalexchange.org.

Slaughterhouses

After slaughtering a few chickens, Mark and I are thankful that we don't do this on a large scale. I am reminded of Old Testament priests who slaughtered sacrificial animals as a routine part of their life, though the sacrifices that the priests carried out were a different kind of killing from what occurs in commercial slaughterhouses. While the system was abused at times, priests were not motivated by profit; their intention was to bind a community together and to God through animals that were cared and tended for and then given up to be consumed in order to contribute to the life of the community.

Truckloads of chickens are driven through our town on their way to slaughter. The sides of the truck are open, so onlookers can see the apathetic birds with dull eyes and deadened spirits packed into wire crates. In the United States, more than eight *billion* chickens a year arrive at slaughter-houses, where they are dumped by the truckload onto a conveyor belt. The only human contact they have is with someone who grabs them by their feet and hangs them upside down onto an overhead conveyor. They pass by a blade intended to slit their throats and then are dipped in the scalding tanks before entering a machine that de-feathers and guts them.

The process is far removed from anything resembling a humane killing or even death at the hands of a human on a family farm. Chickens, it turns out, are exempt from the Humane Slaughter Act.

For a very good reason, slaughterhouses do not have glass walls or offer tours (surely much would change if they did). Nevertheless, I have read accounts of the process and seen some of what transpires on YouTube videos. You, too, can undergo this awful but enlightening experience, thanks to those who want to lift the veil of ignorance for anyone willing to have it lifted.

I've learned that animals are not always killed with the throat-slicing machine or rendered unconscious by the captive bolt pistol (which is shot into the head of cows before slaughtering begins). In the case of larger animals, the worker who shoots the bolt gun knows which animals he fails to kill or render unconscious before the conveyor belt moves them forward to the next station. What must workers do to harden their hearts and souls to this work so that they can feed their families, so that meat can be "affordable," and so that owners can turn a profit? One former slaughterhouse employee described it this way:

> The worst thing, worse than the physical danger, is the emotional toll. If you work in the stick pit [where hogs are killed] for any period of time—that lets you kill things but doesn't let you care. You may look a hog in the eye that's walking around in the blood pit with you and think, "God, that really isn't a bad looking animal." You may want to pet it. Pigs down on the kill floor have come up to nuzzle me like a puppy. Two minutes later I had to kill them. . . . I can't care.[5]

Slaughterhouse workers suffer physical injuries (carpal tunnel syndrome, tendonitis, and other crippling disabilities caused by working fast and re-petitively with various blades), alcoholism (when drinking becomes a coping mechanism), and psychological disorders (from doing a repetitive task that the worker perceives as brutal and alien to his or her nature). Slaughter-house workers are increasingly being treated for PITS (perpetration-induced traumatic stress), a subset of PTSD (post-traumatic stress disorder), which results from having caused and inflicted suffering.[6] One needn't look very far to find a very disturbing and haunting tale of misery, both for the ani-mals being "harvested" in slaughterhouses and those hired to harvest them.

According to the Food Empowerment Project, 38 percent of slaughter-house workers were born outside the United States. An unknown percent are undocumented workers, primarily from Latin American countries. All are low-income workers trying to support themselves and their families.[7] The annual turnover of these jobs ranges from 100 to 250 percent, which means people aren't making it even a year in these jobs. Besides leaving as a result of physical and emotional injuries and exhaustion, those who are migrants leave out of fear or are taken away during raids by immigra-tion officers. Considering the high level of employee turnover, it's not surprising that most slaughterhouses lack motivation to train employees well or to provide safe, pleasant work environments. Those behind the legal efforts to change what goes on in slaughterhouses see it as a chicken-and-egg scenario.

At this point, the ever-increasing demands to improve profit foster the kind of calculation that says it's acceptable when forty birds per shift enter the scalding tank alive, as if such a number can still be considered shy of what "inhumane" would be. Slaughterhouses may keep our meat "affordable," but now that I know something of the profane violence levied against animals and workers in such places I cannot, in good conscience, purchase such meat. Still, it took me a while to consider the problem head-on, though I had suspected for some time that the industry was inhumane. Looking back, I'd say my convictions lived in the realm of abstract philosophy rather than the flesh-and-blood realm of my kitchen.

In *The Invention of Wings*, Sue Monk Kidd tells a story set in the pre–Civil War South. Sarah, one of the main characters, struggles with the fact that her family owns slaves, even as she continues to live a life made possible because of them. At a pivotal point Sarah says, "I saw then what I hadn't seen before, that I was very good at despising slavery in the abstract, in the removed and anonymous masses, but in the concrete, intimate flesh of the girl beside me, I'd lost the ability to be repulsed by it. I'd grown comfortable with the particulars of evil. There's a frightful muteness that dwells at the center of all unspeakable things, and I had found my way into it."[8]

The frightful muteness that dwells at the center of all unspeakable things includes agribusiness. Yet multiple voices are rising, and the muteness is falling away, helping those of us who don't know the true nature of things to understand them for what they are. Supporting humane harvesting practices of all sorts ends up being a remarkably simple way to wade through the complexities of our food system and to pursue justice and extend mercy. Intentionally making those choices makes visible the invisible members of our earthly community, on whom our well-being depends.

At this point you probably would like to hear something hopeful. It's coming. But first I need to introduce Julian of Norwich. I'm sure that some of you already know her.

Julian was a fourteenth-century English mystic, one of many voices who wrote of existential hope and, by doing so, sent it echoing through the centuries. Julian spoke hope into all forms of awfulness. She lived during the Hundred Years' War between England and France and survived the horrors of the bubonic plague that swept across Europe, killing between 30 and 60 percent of Europe's population. She is perhaps most well known for her affirmation, "All shall be well, and all shall be well, and all manner of thing shall be well."[9] But in her seeking, Julian asked God how all could be well when sin had brought so much devastation. The answer was this, written in a language that may sound ancient to our ears yet still resonates with our souls:

> And our blessed Lord answered full meekly and with full lovely cheer, and showed that Adam's sin was the most harm that ever was done, or ever shall be, to the world's end; and our Lord taught that the glorious Amends-making is more pleasing to God and more filled with worth without comparison, than ever was the sin of Adam harmful. Our Lord taught me, "Since I have made well the most harm, then it is my will that you know thereby that I shall make well all that is less."[10]

The fall of humanity is not as bad as the love of God is good. Julian ends the section by recounting that she heard Jesus say "full comfortably: 'I may make all things well, I can make all things well, I will make all things well, and I shall make all thing well; and you shall see yourself that all manner of things shall be well.'"[11]

⤙ *Pursuing Mindfulness* ⤚

When you are ready to learn more about the abuses in our food system, check out the following resources:

Animal rights. Go to the Vegetarian Resource Group for basic definitions, book recommendations, and organizations at vrg.org /nutshell/animalrights.htm.

Farm laborers. Watch the documentary "Food Chains." Access at www.foodchainsfilm.com.

Slaughterhouses. Read Gail Eisnitz's book *Slaughterhouse: The Shocking Story of Greed, Neglect, and Inhumane Treatment inside the US Meat Industry.* For a shorter but more academic piece, read Amy Fitzgerald's article, "A Social History of the Slaughterhouse: From Inception to Contemporary Implications," in *Research in Human Ecology* (humanecologyreview.org/pastissues/her171/Fitz gerald.pdf). You can also google *slaughterhouses* and watch any number of disturbing videos that were secretly filmed of animal abuse. For a bit of good news, watch the life story of Temple Grandin. The movie (*Temple Grandin*) tells the story of a woman with autism who worked to make the design of slaughterhouses more humane in the 1970s and 1980s.

Chocolate. Watch "The Dark Side of Chocolate," a journalistic exploration of the chocolate industry, available on YouTube.

That didn't happen in Julian's lifetime and will not happen in yours and mine. But I share Julian's confidence that eventually all will be made well. That is a great comfort, even if it is primarily an existential one. But the good news doesn't end there.

The Bright Side of Harvesting

Take a deep, cleansing breath and imagine a better world.

That world exists. In places all around the world God is about the business of making things well. People are working toward *shalom*—a peace that comes when justice prevails, when economic choices are based on affection or love rather than profit. An example can be found in Amy Fitzgerald's article about slaughterhouses (see sidebar) that seeks to address slaughterhouse abuses through legal reforms. In many counties across the United States, people can find farms that actually look and act like the charming ones depicted on numerous labels slapped over chicken thighs and breasts in the grocery store.

Carmen Ranch is part of that better world. This eastern Oregon cattle ranch is owned and worked by a fourth-generation rancher, Cory, and her husband, Dave. The Carmens have 150 registered cows between the ages of 2 and 17, and the Carmens know the faces and personalities of each. Calves stay with their mothers from spring through their first autumn; all cows are raised on pasture grass in the summers and fed hay and alfalfa grown and harvested on the Carmen Ranch during the winter. Cory and Dave take on the responsibility of giving their cows a good life and a quick death, with as little stress and pain as possible. To that end, they hire what they describe as a highly skilled artisan who comes to their pasture with his mobile slaughter truck to humanely kill (or harvest) the cows. While the cattle would undoubtedly rather live than die (all living things share the instinct to avoid early death), if I am going to eat meat I want it to come from a steer that died on the same land where he was born and lived out his life.

Since Cory and Dave are committed to ranching in ways that respect the land, animals, and people, they grow hay and alfalfa sustainably, rotate pastures, and do what is required for Carmen cows to be certified grassfed. The certification holds ranchers to rigorous standards of safe and fair working conditions for employees, soil and water conservation, protection of wildlife habitat, and the provision of a healthy and humane life for the animals.[12] People who buy beef from the Carmens purchase, minimally, a quarter of a cow, which includes roasts, steaks, ribs, and hamburger at a little more than six dollars a pound.

Wendell Berry says good stewardship of the land is a matter of scale. We need to keep our work small enough in scale to know our employees' names, to know the animals that we use to our benefit, to know the land, and to know the habits of its other inhabitants. As Berry says, "The right scale in work gives power to affection. When one works beyond the reach of one's love for the place one is working in and for the things and creatures one is working with and among, then destruction inevitably results. An adequate local culture, among other things, keeps work within the reach of love."[13]

Food harvested from places like Carmen Ranch is good food. The sacrifice of the harvest is made sacred by the affectionate care given to the animals from birth to death and the respect given to the workers, the cows, and the land.

For multiple reasons, vegetarians and vegans choose to not eat animals, and vegans also choose to not eat the products of animals. Some do it for their own health. A good number choose it knowing humans don't have to eat meat or dairy or to wear leather or fur to live well, and they don't believe humans should take the lives of feeling, sentient beings merely for the sake of human pleasure. Some vegans and vegetarians might eat meat, cheese, and eggs if the industry were as concerned for ethics and compassion as profit, but they choose not to as a way to stand against dominant practices that cause so much suffering. Some former vegetarians and vegans have returned to eating animal products after gaining access to foods grown and harvested by traditional practices of compassionate animal husbandry, which provide an alternative to profit-driven modern food systems.

Sarah, our daughter, has been a vegan for nine years now. She has chosen to be a witness-bearer to the dark side of harvesting animals, yet she does so in an inviting and life-giving way. She went to culinary school to learn the French art of baking pastries and now invites readers into the healthy, tasty, compassionate world of vegan food through her popular food blog, *My Darling Vegan*. I have learned much from her commitment to animal rights ethics and how that stance drives her choices.

Eating ethically requires mindfulness. It is less convenient and not always available; in addition, one pays more for naturally grown produce and compassionately raised and slaughtered meat because harvesting responsibly involves intensive work that can't be done quickly. Indeed, much of the tending and harvesting is done by hand. We, like the farmers at most family-run organic farms, pick slugs off lettuce we've just harvested and smash cucumber beetles copulating on squash blossoms between our fingers while picking zucchini, crookneck, and tromboncino squash.

The food tastes better. The food *is* better—for the body and the soul, for neighbors near and far. Because we farm on a small scale, we know the land and some of its inhabitants. We know which rock walls the king and garter snakes particularly like for nesting and where we will likely come across one in the strawberry patch or find one resting in the shade of the marionberry and raspberry bushes. Yes, snakes startle me a bit when I happen on them unawares, but since I know they are harmless to me, I like to occasionally pick one up and let it slide between my fingers and around my wrist, a more-cool-than-warm rubbery being, smooth, strong, and so very full of life. He or she is probably also full of fear. So I don't hold them often, or for long.

The point is, I know that this place is their home, just as it is mine. They are among my many, many neighbors, and they are particularly helpful at keeping mice and voles out of the garden. We know which birds will be after the corn and peas when they first emerge from the dirt. We know the stories of our apprentices and get to know the names of the children who come to pick up produce with their moms and/or dads each week. The scale of our endeavor allows affection to drive our choices.

Wendell Berry's statement that scale is an important part of affection— that knowing a place and each animal makes it easier to care well and to be a good farmer or a good rancher—made me think again about what we as a society lost as we transitioned from small- to large-scale farming. We exchanged hoes and hands for tractors and combines and moved from killing chickens in our backyards to killing them on conveyor belts. In the process we lost affection for the land, laborers of the land, and animals.

Still, I believe that one day all will be well, and that all *is* being made well through a resurgence of interest and enthusiasm for local economies and local foods. Fern Creek is just one of thousands of farms that harvest affection through labors of love.

Harvesting Affection

One of the crops Mark and I harvest every year is honey. We keep four hives—Emma, Lucy, Grace, and June. Being "keepers of bees" exaggerates the ownership component of sharing one's space with bees. What it mostly means is that we put together boxes filled with wax foundation frames and "invite" bees to make a home among us by dumping a bunch of bees (including a queen) into the box. Generally they accept the offer, though they send off swarms to populate the world elsewhere.

Different queens and different worker bees and drones have inhabited those hive boxes over the years, and we live in a contented coexistence with each other. We supply them with an ideal part-sun/part-shade location, a windbreak from the west, a good water supply, and ample access to thousands of flowers and buds from thousands of different plants. In exchange they supply us with honey, though they don't understand this arrangement up front. We only take the extra honey we are sure that they will not need to survive the winter. From their point of view, they are not so sure.

This year we had a perfect spring and summer, and when we harvested, the frames were heavy with honey. After spinning it out, we filled quarts and pints with twenty-seven gallons of a honey so clear and light it tasted like spring. We try to be gentle and as unobtrusive as possible because we know this theft feels disastrous to a hive; we return emptied frames to the hive, giving the bees a chance to reclaim the residual honey.

These are such little creatures, and not, according to most accounts, sentient. Yet I wish I could thank the bees and assure them that we have left them enough.

Sometimes the affection and worry I have for the bees feels childlike. But maybe this kind of childlikeness is what God calls us to, reminding us of simple connections to God's creation and creatures that are not complicated by efficiency and profit.

Sacrifice is involved in any honey harvest. I want it to deepen my appreciation for the sweet nectar of the bees that live on Fern Creek. We celebrate with our traditional biscuits and honey supper, accompanied by a salad that is meant to keep us from overeating the biscuits and honey. We gave a jar of the golden nectar to our apprentices in the basement, jars to the bakers at Newberg Bakery who supply us with bread for our CSA, and a jar to the woman who tends my farmer-weary-worn body with a massage every four to six weeks. Most of this honey is sold to members of our CSA and to local folks who drive out to Fern Creek for it. With every jar I want to send home a bit of Fern Creek affection, a sacred sacrifice that makes its way into the homes, kitchens, and bodies of people in my community.

Those of us living in the Global North (the "industrialized" or "post-industrial" world) are beginning again to harvest all kinds of food for ourselves and for our neighbors. We are harvesting honey, eggs, fruits, and vegetables, and in doing so, we join those in the Global South who never stopped tending creatures and plants.

Abundance and access to food are part of the Global North food ethic. We want lots of food, and generally we want it to be affordable for all people. For the most part, we have accomplished that goal. Still, if abundance and access are the only aspects of our ethic, we miss other important dimensions of eating well. Agribusiness doesn't want us to pay attention to how our food gets to us because another way—a more ethical way—will interfere with profit. Agribusiness spokespeople are probably right in thinking that most people don't want to know anyway, especially if raising and harvesting food differently means it would cost more.

A food ethic that includes knowing something about the harvesting process adds an important element. The more we know, the more ethically we can choose to eat. And yet, while knowing more about where our food comes from and how it is harvested is better than just valuing abundance and access, ethical eating comes full circle when it draws us toward affection. Affectionate eating calls us to love God, neighbor, and creation through the daily choices we make that are related to food. When harvesting practices are defined by compassion, justice, and good stewardship, we heal broken parts of the world, coaxing out a healthier land, healthier animals, healthier laborers and, it turns out, healthier selves.

All is being made well as people participate in opportunities to harvest their own food or support the good work of harvesting done by farmers and ordinary folk in their neighborhoods, communities, and towns.

• Sarah's Quinoa-Stuffed Acorn Squash •

The year my daughter Sarah (of *My Darling Vegan*) belonged to our CSA she'd post a recipe every week that used produce from her crate. This was one of my fall-time favorites.

3   acorn squash, cut in half

1   large apple, peeled and diced

1 tbsp.   olive oil

1 tbsp.	fresh or 1 tsp. dried sage
½ c.	red quinoa
3 c.	pecans, chopped
1 c.	vegetable broth or water
	salt and pepper
1	small red onion
½ c.	vegan mozzarella cheese (Sarah uses Diaya)

Preheat oven to 375 degrees. Cut acorn squash in half (lengthwise) and scoop out the seeds. Place cut side down on a baking dish and bake for 30 minutes.

Meanwhile, prepare the quinoa. Thoroughly rinse and drain (to remove quinoa's naturally bitter coat). Heat a small pan over medium heat and add quinoa. Toast the grain, stirring constantly for one minute. Add 1 cup of vegetable broth (or water) and bring to a boil. Reduce heat to low and cover for 15 minutes. Remove from heat and keep covered for an additional 5 minutes.

In a separate pan, heat 1 tablespoon oil over medium-high heat. Add diced onions and sauté until translucent (about 5 minutes). Add pecans and apples and sauté for another 3–5 minutes. Add sage, stir together, and remove from heat. Combine apple/onion mixture with cooked quinoa and add salt and pepper to taste.

Remove acorn squash from oven and carefully flip over so that they are cut side up. Scoop quinoa mixture into the squash, stuffing in as much as you can. Cover each squash with aluminum foil and return to oven for another 20–30 minutes until squash is tender.

Carefully remove aluminum foil and evenly top with vegan cheese. Return to oven for 3–5 minutes until cheese has melted. Remove, and let cool slightly.

Reflections and Questions

1. List multiple ways you experience abundance. Reflect on or talk about how readily you connect abundance to gratitude. What might encourage you to do this more automatically?

2. A significant issue related to good animal husbandry and fair labor practices is the capacity of people on low or fixed incomes to pay

for food from sources using these practices. Brainstorm (ideally with others) options that could be made available in your community or church to assist people on limited budgets to eat more compassionately and justly.

3. Have you had any experience (directly or indirectly, through a family member or friend) with killing animals, including hunting or fishing? What is that like for you, and how does reading the story of slaughtering roosters affect you? What experiences, or lack of experiences, contribute to how you respond as you do?

4. Reflect on the distinction between sacred and profane violence. Do you find it a helpful distinction in the conversation about how the animals we eat are raised and slaughtered? How so? If not, explain.

5. The Bible is full of animal husbandry stories. Consider the following parables and proverb, reflecting on them not only in terms of spiritual truth but also for what they teach us about how caring for animals was understood in biblical times: John 10:1–16 (story of the Good Shepherd), Luke 15:1–7 (parable of the lost sheep), and Proverbs 12:10 ("A righteous man cares for the needs of his animal, but the kindest acts of the wicked are cruel" [NIV]).

6. Consider challenging yourself to make the commitment to purchase one food item from ethical sources. Bananas, coffee, and chocolate are a good place to start. Coca-Cola is an example of a product you might choose to stop consuming altogether once you look into the corporation's water practices here and abroad. Start with the village of Mehdiganj in India.

7. When seen through the lens of history, evil is both easier and more comfortable to identify. Consequently, people tend to recognize the great social evils perpetrated by their nation after the fact. We are often reminded of the astounding human ability to justify whatever we are doing. What makes it easy to not see some of our current food practices as immoral? What makes it easy to grow "comfortable with the particulars of evil" that reside in parts of agribusiness? Will identifying the places of injustice and suffering be enough to eventually change the food industry? If not, what kinds of barriers might need to be overcome, and what might help people see

through their ways of justifying participation in the darker sides of agribusiness?

8. Sit with Julian of Norwich's claim that all will be well. Knowing we won't see everything made well in our lifetime, does her fourteenth-century proclamation inspire you more to action or to a complacent acceptance of the way things are? Why do you think so?

6
In the Garden

Praise the LORD, I tell myself. . . .
You send rain on the mountains from your heavenly home,
   and you fill the earth with the fruit of your labor.
You cause grass to grow for the cattle,
   You cause plants to grow for people to use.
   You allow them to produce food from the earth—
   wine to make them glad,
   olive oil as lotion for their skin,
   and bread to give them strength. . . .
O Lord, what a variety of things you have made!
   In wisdom you have made them all.
   The earth is full of your creatures. . . .
As for me—I will praise the LORD!
Praise the LORD!

—Psalm 104:1, 13–15, 24, 35b NLT 1996

Most evenings during the summer, Mark and I take our supper out to the courtyard. In July when the red crocosmia stalks rise from the ground, opening bloom by bloom to the tip of each stalk, hummingbirds join us. Ruby-throated hummingbirds and Anna's hummingbirds dine six feet away, supping alongside us, as it were. We planted those crocosmia several years ago and take no small pleasure in seeing hummingbirds feed on their trumpet-shaped blossoms.

These suppers are a mini-Sabbath of sorts. We rest from our labor in the gardens and fields, acknowledging that good work has been done this day. There is nowhere else we'd rather be and nothing else we need to be doing. According to Norman Wirzba, observation of the Sabbath was historically understood as "learning to rest in God's generous goodness and receive the world as a gift."[1]

According to this definition, it seems that we are observing a Sabbath rest in those moments at the end of the day. Later, Wirzba writes:

God's first *Shabbat* was the occasion for complete rest and delight in a world of creatures wonderfully and beautifully made. In a Sabbath world there should be no exploitation or hoarding. . . . Instead there should be the joy of knowing that the world is sustained and loved into being by the God who is continually pouring and emptying himself out for creation's good. There is gratitude and affirmation, a genuine cherishing of the gifts of God. The realization of Sabbath, in other words, is also the realization of a genuine feast.[2]

Like many Christians, I tend to associate Sabbath with a day off, which usually involves a church service and an afternoon nap. Truth is, other than the church service, I've never taken this sort of Sabbath seriously. It seems optional, like fasting, which I also don't take seriously. It's hard to take a day of intentional rest when I live in a culture that is proud of how much productivity and economic activity can be squeezed out of every day. But throughout my adult life, various writers have helped me to reconsider Sabbath.[3] Most recently, Wirzba has offered me a new paradigm that helps me understand that Sabbath is more than a forced day off. I've been challenged to sit with the humbling thought that humans were *not* the final act of creation; the final act was God stopping to savor the goodness and harmony of creation in its fullness. The Jewish people were commanded to take a day every week to do the same. It helped keep them collectively and individually aware of their dependence on God and of the soul's need to turn toward gratitude. They, like us, needed (and need) to stop laboring and observe the wonder that comes when sun, water, dirt, plants, insects, animals, and people work together. What good might emerge if collectively we paused to savor the goodness and then praised God together for this manifestation of attentive love?

Understanding the Sabbath as a time to usher in stillness so that we can pay attention, acknowledge our dependence, and praise may be easier when our work is physically challenging and creatively engages the natural world rather than when it takes place in offices or buildings. Spending all of our days and nights inside buildings can make it difficult to remember that our primary home, our place of sustenance, is the one outside the walls we build to keep cold and heat, rain and wind, and mice and raccoons at bay. Living inside buildings may be our reality, but it's also an obstacle that keeps us from stopping and savoring the wonder of God's creation. From inside or outside, the Sabbath calls us to pause from our work—that is, from our various manipulations of creation—in order to glory in how it all works and to savor the work we have done. In the savoring, we honor God, who made it all possible and makes it possible still.

Such a picture draws me in, inviting me to a Sabbath rest that centers and grounds my soul.

As I relish the hummingbirds feasting from crocosmia blossoms in the courtyard and the squirrels climbing and jumping from tree to tree overhead while I lie in the hammock, as I inhale the fragrance of lilacs and honeysuckle and basil and rosemary when I stroll the gardens in the evening, I love to imagine God doing the same. When we find ways to do this individually and collectively, we worship and honor the Creator of life. We remember, thank, and praise the One on whom we depend for life.

Maybe it's good and right that during those suppers in the courtyard I can't help but make happy noises as I eat. "Hmms" tumble out of my mouth like freshly picked blueberries poured from pail to serving bowl. Mark smiles and sometimes joins me in my visceral and verbal appreciation of good food grown and gathered from the gardens and cooked in the kitchen.

As though it is unusual, we make note that the food on our plates had been growing in the garden just hours before—or in the case of dilly beans and tomato sauce, in the season prior, grown within seventy-five yards of our table. In this Sabbath-like space we are quieted enough to notice and delight in the feeding hummingbirds, the evening breeze on our faces, and the cackling conversation of hens.

In case I have painted too idyllic a picture, let me clarify: it's not like I just go out to the gardens and pluck a tomato and tromboncino squash for dinner. Well, it is and it isn't like that. At some points in the season, it is a lot like that. But the work required to get to that point is hard—tedious, stressful, and worrisome work.

For instance, this spring the mice ate nearly all the Blue Lake pole and yellow wax beans before they had a chance to sprout. Rain and slugs took out a good chunk of our strawberry crop, and a raccoon managed to climb a tree near the deer fence, hop over (or so we assumed by the foot-prints), and wreak havoc on the newly planted eggplants, pulling them up and tossing them like weeds in the path between our freshly weeded beds. Trying to grow food is discouraging sometimes. Our apprentices get to see Mark and my marriage in its most raw state in May, experienced through grumpy and agitated lives when our tendency to blame the other for life's woes is never far from our lips.

Yet *all* of it can be soul forming. Mark and I are humbled by how easily we, two generally centered Quaker souls, can get off-kilter. We are reminded of the importance of apologizing, holding our tongue, seeking forgiveness, and forgiving. Each morning we gather with our apprentices and read a prayer, generally one of two from Forward Movement.[4] One recent May day we read the following prayer from Phillip Brooks with particular awareness of its appropriateness:

> O God: Give me strength to live another day; Let me not turn coward before its difficulties or prove recreant to its duties; Let me not lose faith in other people; Keep me sweet and sound of heart, in spite of ingratitude, treachery, or meanness; Preserve me from minding little stings or giving them; Help me to keep my heart clean, and to live so honestly and fearlessly that no outward failure can dishearten me or take away the joy of conscious integrity; Open wide the eyes of my soul that I may see good in all things; Grant me this day some new vision of thy truth; Inspire me with the spirit of joy and gladness; and make me the cup of strength to suffering souls; in the name of the strong Deliverer, our only Lord and Savior, Jesus Christ.[5]

And so it is through hardship and abundance that Mark and I draw nearest to the source of our sustenance in the Fern Creek fields. Might we be closest to our first calling as tillers of the soil and stewards of the land when we cultivate our homeplace, bringing forth food for ourselves and for those with whom we live, in sickness and health, through hard times and easy ones?

I'm not suggesting that everyone go out and buy a micro-farm, work long hours, and plant hummingbird-attracting plants. Instead, I'm calling us to a place of awareness of God's providence in the ordinariness of life, in both easy times and hard ones. Perhaps the most ordinary reminder we have is the food we eat multiple times a day. Maybe you will get inspired to start a small salsa garden if you have space in the backyard or add a planter for tomatoes on the porch. Maybe this awareness will grow in you a deeper appreciation of the fact that food comes from someplace else and requires some measure of work before it gets to the supermarket.

Good things happen as a result of working a garden—good, soul-forming things. Although there are probably hundreds, I'll just mention seven evidences of God's daily grace in the garden. These good things can happen when any of us grows food in our backyard or on our rooftop; they are life and gardening lessons, which often enough are one and the same.

Good Thing #1: Gardening Answers Our Call to Cultivate and Be Stewards of Our Home

A kind of magic happens when people put their creativity and affection for a place to good use. Meditative Japanese gardens emerge, as well as countryside vineyards, English gardens, peach orchards, and CSA (community supported agriculture) farms. Stay with me as I "wax historical," as my friend Allison says. I want to tell you a gardening story.

A little more than a hundred years ago, Robert Pim Butchart owned some land in Victoria, British Columbia, that he mined for limestone. He built a quarry and made cement to meet the demand in cities along the West Coast, from San Francisco to Portland. After he exhausted the land, his wife, Jennie, decided to reclaim the vast pit they'd gouged out of the earth. She had cartloads of topsoil brought in and began to grow flowers and create flourishing spaces in what came to be known as the Butchart Gardens. Robert loved her vision and, inspired by his own love of exotic birds, added ducks and a duck pond, peacocks for the front lawn, and artsy birdhouses throughout the gardens. Some of the other spaces in Butchart Gardens include the Italian Garden, the Rose Garden, and the Japanese Garden on the seaside. Nearly a million people visit this destination every year.

Jennie had a vision to take land that had been devastated and to heal it, creating something unique and beautiful.

Throughout history, humans have almost always cultivated land, partnering with it in some way particular to their culture and time. Mostly we cultivate land to make food more predictable and easier to access, but sometimes we do it simply to create beauty. When farming is done well by someone who has affection for the place being worked, function and beauty come together. Marigold flowers planted among the beans and cabbage blend function and beauty. Add a pole bean teepee built between the onion patch and the summer squash and whimsy gets tossed into the mix, inviting children and adults alike to sit or lie on the straw-covered floor and take a Sabbath moment to be charmed by the green-dappled shade. If one is thankful for fast-growing vines that provide shade and a midday snack, one might well be worshiping the God who made it so.

When people partner well—that is, when they grow food, forage, fish, and hunt, when they take trees from forests and rocks from the ground in ways that are good for the land and good for the animals and people of the land—they are good stewards. Their work honors the Creator, who ordains, blesses, and sustains these earthy relationships between people and the places they live.

Whimsical gardens, orderly gardens, and the range of intentionally cultivated gardens that lie between express affection for the land and perhaps a humble relationship between the steward who works the land and the land that responds with flowers, food, drink, and beauty.

Good Thing #2: Gardening Provides Good and Meaningful Labor

People who knew us as college professors sometimes look askance at our decision to . . . what? Tend a large garden? They are confused and cannot understand why an intelligent woman would exchange a vibrant and rewarding academic life for unrewarded manual labor. They are perplexed that Mark would take all the discretionary time he has to grow food for others, though not in a way that replaces lost income from my up and quitting a "real" job. I imagine they think our farm labor is beneath us, that it underutilizes our potential to make a difference in the world.

This is what I want to say to people who cannot understand poorly paid, low-status manual labor: *Work that meets a basic need, engages a person in relationships (even with soil, plants, bees, and other farmers), requires skill, and fosters creativity has its rewards.* Since the scope of our work is small enough that we know the land, our fellow laborers, and the people who eat our produce, we have a community that nourishes and feeds our souls. For the record, this kind of work is not limited to farming. Is it not also true of mothering and of volunteer or poorly paid work done in communities around the world?

In the 1960s and 1970s, students from Eliot Wigginton's ninth- and tenth-grade English classes in an Appalachian school interviewed aging folks who had lived out their lives in the mountains of north Georgia.

Students took down instructions for how to make things as varied as fiddles and tar, and they got a glimpse into the hearts and souls of ordinary people who lived simply off the land. Annie Perry, an eighty-three-year-old woman and one of the people interviewed, had much to say about work in the garden:

> When you live in the country, you can have a garden and you can go pick fresh vegetables when you want 'em, and they don't cost you so much. God gives you the strength and if you use what He gave you, you might not make a bountiful crop, but you can make some. If you've lived long enough and nobody won't hire you and you're able to work, you can make you something to eat, and you can eat it. . . . I think everybody should work. We're all put here to work. We are all put here to make a living by the sweat of our brows. . . . Work keeps people's minds occupied and keeps 'em from doing things they're not supposed to do. If they got their minds on their work, they'll be successful.[6]

I imagine that another thing Annie Perry had, and maybe something she took for granted, was a fair bit of flexibility and a lot of variety in her day-to-day routines. I have the same, which is worth a lot to me. If it's a rainy day, I can go upstairs to my office and write instead of weeding the herb garden and clipping up the tomatoes. True, on a pickup day we will harvest in rain or 100-degree heat, but on such days we will be rewarded with an appreciative community who will commiserate and thank us, who may have thought of us during the morning harvest, and who will value their crate of food all the more.

Our ethics, mission, and love of God, land, and others drive how we grow our food and what we do with it. We honor God and our neighbors and neighborhood when our work is ethical and missional. When we have extra yellow beans, I get to choose whether or not to sell them to a local restaurant, donate them to Friendsview Retirement Community, drop them off at our local food bank, or feed them to the chickens and the compost bin. All of those options are neighborly, and the freedom to choose what to do with the excess is part of good work.

One doesn't have to make money at a thing for it to be good work, nor does the work associated with food require one to quit a paying job. Keeping a home garden can also be good and meaningful. Work is good when it recognizes and honors our dependence on the earth, fosters collaborative relationships with other members of creation, uses our God-given creativity, and grants us freedom to choose how we work and what we do with the fruits of our labors.

This is the opposite of work that alienates us from creation, causing us to use the things of earth to satisfy our hungers without thought to the cost and harm for other members of creation. Alienating work tends to define relationships with others in terms of competition—we compete for recognition, for promotions, or for consumers. Sometimes work alienates us from our own selves, requiring us to dull our creativity and simply do what we are told in the way we are told to do it. Some work dulls our conscience, and we begin to think our work is okay because it provides a necessary paycheck for ourselves or our family, even if it is not meaningful and does not contribute to the well-being of others. What good might come if, as Christian communities, we helped each other think about meaningful work, about balancing vocation with pragmatics, about our sense of home and rootedness, and about our tendency to overvalue achievement?

Not everyone has access to good work. Humanity has always struggled to create the kinds of economic and political systems that give everyone access to good work. Maybe it is idealistic to hope for it this side of heaven, but then again, maybe keeping a vegetable garden is one way to experience some of the goodness that is absent in many workplaces.

Good Thing #3: Failure Is Okay, Expected, and a Good Teacher Besides

I composted thirty pounds of big Yukon Gold potatoes last year. We had harvested them and put them on racks to dry on the shady porch for several days before storing them for later distribution. Here's what I learned: it is not *direct* sunlight that turns potatoes green (which is what I assumed); it is simply *light*. When I pulled out those potatoes, they had that sickly green tinge that told me they were only good for composting. I wouldn't even feed them to the chickens because that green tinge bespeaks a toxin that is harmful to humans, so presumably it is harmful to hens as well. Come to think of it, I hope I didn't poison our compost pile.

At any rate, hard lesson, that—and one I won't forget.

We have had dozens of such lessons over the thirty-five years that we have grown vegetables and fruits, but most of them happened in the last six years, when we went from growing about seven crops to more than seventy-five. Since we grow without using herbicides, pesticides, or petroleum-based fertilizers (all of which help manage certain troubles rather easily), it means we've had an awful lot to learn.

Here's another example. Some of our plants start life inside, under grow lights in the dark of winter. Others start life outside, from seeds planted when the soil temperature is warm enough to encourage sprouting and quick growth. We've learned that plants need to start strong to do well. If we put little seedlings in the ground and all they get is cold rain for several weeks, they don't grow. They bravely try hunkering down to wait out the storm, but in the meantime, the cabbage root fly emerges ready for sex and reproduction. Once the females have flown their nuptial flights, they (smartly) look for tender young plants and lay their eggs at the base. The maggots hatch to a ready feast—tender roots of tasty broccoli, cabbage, and kale.

From our failures we learned that an established plant can handle nibbles but a young one cannot. How else might we learn such a lesson? Some mistakes we can avoid by deducing, but when it comes to growing plants, experience is a good teacher, even if sometimes a harsh one. Still, we have avoided mistakes by reading, talking with other farmers, and sitting at the feet of various teachers.

Even if failure can be a good teacher, we'd rather avoid the worst mistakes in life (and in the garden). Apprenticing oneself to a wiser, older soul helps. By hearing another's stories, we can (hopefully) learn from his or her mistakes.

Maybe the phrase "saved from our sin" ought to be large enough to include being saved from making the worst mistakes. Sometimes we make little ones, which help us avoid the big ones. Sometimes we are saved through God's guidance, which is mediated through parents, teachers, friends, communities of faith, and the law. Strengthening these social bonds helps us choose well.

Mistakes are going to happen both in and out of the garden. If we can learn from them, we are better served than if we find a way to blame the weather or fate or our comrades. I find it comforting to remember that all mistakes have been made before. Thank God for grace—including the grace of mistakes that help us find a way forward.

❧ *Planting Seedlings So They Grow Strong* ❧

I have put healthy-looking broccoli, basil, and tomatoes in the ground and watched them die. They wilted at the first heat wave or swooned with the first cold snap. When they came from a nursery, I suspected foul play rather than my own ineptitude.

Once I confronted my ineptitude, it wasn't that hard to learn what I needed to know to successfully move plants from cartons in a greenhouse to the garden dirt outside. It helps to see the transition from the plant's perspective. So far it has been watered when thirsty—no more, no less. It's had 12–16 hours of light (but not direct sunlight) in a room with a temperature that's 60–70 degrees. Suddenly it's whisked outside, dumped from a cozy cell, and plopped in cold, wet dirt. The temperature may dip near or below freezing by night, and the sun's fury beats down by day. Hardly an easy transition.

Seedlings need to be toughened up before they can survive the real world. Once one understands that, the rest is relatively easy. Here's how we transition seedlings to the garden.

1. Plant them at the right time. Just because the stores are selling tomatoes, peppers, and basil in May doesn't mean it's warm enough to plant them outside. Check a planting calendar for your zone, and don't be in a hurry to plant too soon.

2. Harden off seedlings before planting them outside by placing them where they will get a few hours of direct sun for a day or two. Ideally, move them a bit more into the sun for a couple more days. If the night temperatures drop close to or below 40 degrees, move them into the garage. We use a couple of cold frames, which are essentially wood boxes Mark constructed with a glass window that fits on top, so that we can transition our seedlings with less need to babysit them. We take off or prop open the window during the day and close it up at night.

3. While hardening off seedlings, work the area where they will be planted. Loosen up the soil and get rid of competing weeds. Consider raised beds, which are wonderful for backyard gardens.

Besides being attractive, they make both weed control and harvesting easier.

4. Once the seedlings have been hardened off they can be planted. Gather a pail for water, a pint or quart container for scooping water, a hand trowel, and some fertilizer. I add gloves, a kneeling pad, and a mocha.

5. Dig holes for each plant that are 5–6 inches deep, 3–4 inches around, and about 12–18 inches apart. The distance varies depending on the vegetable, but cabbages, broccoli, tomatoes, and peppers can all be planted at about this spacing; lettuce can be closer. The bigger the plant and the more it spreads out, the more space it will need. Pumpkins can grow into nice big jack-o'-lanterns if they have 5–8 feet between rows. Plants usually come with some sort of planting instructions; if not, that information is available on internet gardening sites.

6. If using an organic fertilizer, which will have less nitrogen than conventional petroleum-based fertilizer, add ⅓ – ½ cup to each hole. Otherwise, follow the directions on the package for how much to use. Mix and chop the fertilizer into the hole, which enlarges it as dirt from the sides gets blended in.

7. Use your fist to create a flat, solid base for the roots. Tamping the soil lightly reestablishes a capillary bed so water doesn't move through the loose dirt too quickly, making it difficult for the roots to take up nutrients.

8. Remove the seedling from whatever container it's in, handling it by the root-ball or the leaves. *Don't hold it by the stem*, which is akin to putting a stranglehold on a tender, fragile plant. Place the seedling in the hole and pour a pint or two of water around it, creating a muddy slurry. Pull in dirt from the sides and pat it around the plant. Water the seedling with another pint or two (depending on the wetness of the dirt and the size of the hole). It's okay if it looks quite wet at first—though if the plant is drowning in water a couple of minutes later, use less water next time.

9. Sit back on your heels, take a sip of your mocha, greet the bee that flies by, and move on.

A few notes: New seedlings need more frequent watering than established ones. Seedlings also need to get their roots down into the soil, so only water daily if you've planted during a particular hot spell, then transition to 2–3 times a week. Most plants should get about an inch of water per week and can be watered once or twice a week once established. Since the plant is getting its roots established in the first week, don't be alarmed if nothing happens aboveground for a week or so or if the plants look wilted the first couple of days after planting. Give them a chance to live.

Good Thing #4: We See the Interconnection of Things and Our Place within Creation

Here's what I learned about dung beetles this summer. They live on every continent except Antarctica. They are called "dung" beetles because they take poop from animals that graze on grass (mostly) and roll it into balls the size of a golf ball. What they *don't do* with these dung balls is push them down a hill to smash their enemies or build walls around their homestead. What they *do* is eat them. Dung balls supply all the beetles need in terms of nutrition; they don't even need water to chase it down. Dung beetles prefer poop from herbivores like cows and kangaroos, but in a pinch they'll take what they can get. One or two beetles roll dung into a ball and then roll it to their destination, using the sun by day and the Milky Way by night to help them go in a straight line away from the dung pile, since they want to avoid other beetles who may want to steal their ball. Different species (there are about six thousand of them—I'm telling you, I learned a fair bit, being rather fascinated with these feces-loving creatures) deviate somewhat on their destination, but they all agree on the dung ball's value as a food supply for themselves and their babies.

These beneficial insects fit into our interdependently connected creation rather nicely. By removing poop they reduce the poop-loving fly population, a species that spreads disease to humans by visiting our food after tumbling around in various piles of animal manure. Flies are food for other insects, bats, and birds, so even they have their place in creation, though I somewhat loathe admitting it.

Gardening helps one to pay attention to things like dung beetles and to think about how individual pieces fit in the big scheme of things. To see dung beetles and become fascinated by them and then to read about dung beetles and become more fascinated—might that be a kind of love affair with the wonders of an interconnected world? Everything, even flies, has a place in the food chain.

The longer I've gardened, the more I've come to see that all living things have three activities in common: eating, procreating, and relishing—although some might argue with me on the relishing part. I've said enough about eating. The procreation part you can imagine easily enough. People, rabbits, flies, plants—they all want to propagate and *need* to propagate for the sake of their kind. Dandelions send fluffy seeds on the wind, and the thorny eggplant husk discourages eaters from taking every fruit off the plant, ensuring adequate seed will fall to the soil to be nourished for the next generation. Cucumber beetles copulate in the blossoms of squash and cucumber plants, and the swooping and squawking of robins chasing off a hawk (or me!) when it (or I) gets too near their nest of babies shows that robins will take on giants to protect their own.

We hear less about the strength of life's desire to relish, to take pleasure in, and to savor life itself. Yet for the observer who pays attention, relishing unfolds every day everywhere. Hear the morning and evening birdsong; see the bees cluster on the front of their hive box—a phenomenon beekeepers call "bearding"—which happens on hot summer evenings when their nectar-gathering work is done. Observe cows let loose in the first spring pasture; they literally kick up their heels with delight. And look! See how the goats play, how the hens bask in the sun!

Pollifax, our cat, sometimes joins me in the hammock in the late afternoon when I'm done with my work, and his purr vibrates my stomach. What is purring, if not an embodied form of relishing the present moment? In that hammock at the end of the day, I look for the dappled sun coming through the leaves and the squirrel that plays in the trees sometimes. I listen to the creek and note the weightlessness of my swaying body. In my most attentive moments those thoughts take me to God and a thankfulness that God sustains a world that continues—millennia after millennia—to provide food, life that reproduces and nurtures the next generation, sustaining a world chock-full of delight.

It makes me want to do my part to be a good gardener and a good steward who loves as God does. Working in a garden gives me a part to play. I am one of earth's cultivators, yes, but more than that, I am a witness to astonishing things that happen in a garden, a witness with language to tell what I find so astonishing, to invite others to look and see for themselves.

I am but one species that eats, wants my offspring to flourish, and hopes for a good life filled with simple pleasures. But our species is powerful, and our choices have consequences on the quality of life for other, far less powerful beings. My choices as a gardener and my choices as a consumer matter. Working in the garden has helped me see these interconnected webs of life more clearly.

Good Thing #5: We Learn Tenacity and Hope

A rooster has tenacity, and who knows, maybe hope as well. On a mid-August morning, my four-year-old granddaughter Juniper and I sat outside eating. We ate oatmeal made better by a Chehalis apple that had fallen from a tree, a dash of cinnamon, a pinch of nutmeg, and a spoonful of brown sugar. A rooster down the road crowed, and Juniper looked at me and said, "It's a rooster!" The rooster crowed again.

And again.

Juniper found his call rather delightful, but she eventually asked, "Why does he keep crowing?"

"Maybe because he is glad for the new day," I said.

She thought and then said, "And maybe to wake up his friends."

Tenacity and hope—roosters express it, as do cucumber and flea beetles. At least they express tenacity, but I like to imagine that hope motivates them as well, that what they long and hunger for can be realized if they tenaciously keep on.

So it is with those who work with plants in gardens.

Gardeners need tenacity to hoe down weeds that want to outcompete young plants. They do so because of the hope that these young plants will one day yield pounds of tomatoes or a dozen peppers or perhaps one delectable head of cauliflower.

We need tenacity to ward off other creatures—like cabbage maggots, slugs, and aphids—that want to consume what we are working to grow to feed ourselves. We look for viruses, fungi, and bottom rot and are diligent to catch early and attempt to stop what we can, what could take down a whole crop.

Fortunately we have help, such as ladybugs that eat aphids, and sunshine, water, and healthy soil that help plants grow fast so they can stand a bit of nibbling from beneath or above. When I see ladybugs on the dill, I am mostly happy because help has arrived in the garden. I'm only *mostly* happy because the presence of ladybugs means we probably also have aphids.

We call the creatures that eat what we want to eat "pests" and plants that grow where we don't want them to grow "weeds." Tenacity helps us keep these unwanted residents from overwhelming a garden.

Weeds, if they are controlled at all, are controlled in one of two ways. The more common method is relatively easy and has become the standard practice for keepers of lawns and flowers, as well as growers of food: spray herbicide to poison the plants. Herbicides can be specifically brewed to kill a wide spectrum of plants, or they can be more narrowly focused on something like broadleaf plants. The other practice used throughout history until roughly the mid-twentieth century requires the physical removal of weeds by hoeing, cultivating with a plow, or hand pulling—all of which require tenacity on a deeper, more humble level.

Mark is the most tenacious hoer at Fern Creek. He will rise early and get a start on it, partly because he is the most thorough and the quickest at it but also because he says he likes hoeing. He finds a garden free of weeds aesthetically pleasing, but he also values the physical reminder of weeds in his life that need hoeing. I love how easily the one form of hoeing calls forth the other. It inspires me to pay more attention, calling forth my own need to eradicate weeds. Weeding can remind gardeners to think about what competes for space in our lives, for nutrients that would help us grow more fully into who we are created to be as beings who are seeded with God's image. Trash television comes to mind, which isn't something I watch often, but I watch it often enough that I know what it is to be drawn into a world that neither inspires me toward beauty and honor nor gives me hope in the world.

A gardener soon learns that "pests" also need tenacious oversight. They can be managed in at least four ways that don't interfere to a great extent with the interconnection of things and one way that messes with it mightily on several levels. The first method is to purchase carnivorous ladybugs and lacewings and introduce them to the fields (where they will commence eating unsuspecting vegetarian pests) and to plant flowers that will draw both pollinating and carnivorous insects. We employ this method liberally, which gives Fern Creek a somewhat whimsical appearance as marigolds planted throughout the gardens, and sunflowers and zinnias planted along the fences, flash "Welcome! Vacancy!" signs for beneficial insects.

A second method is to put up some kind of barrier to keep pests out. Game fence keeps deer out fairly effectively, and row covers keep birds from eating newly sprouted beans and corn and keep flea beetles from consuming kale and cabbage.

A third method is to scare pests away. Old CDs strung over blueberries and newly planted beans help keep birds away. The Smashing Pumpkins and Red Hot Chili Peppers might be particularly appropriate, although since the music isn't actually played, the Beatles or Chicago would flash in the sun with the summer breeze just as well. For the record, we've found that barriers work better than CDs.

Fourth, one can kill pests outright, but selectively, killing only the pest that is eating the produce rather than all the insects in the vicinity. For us this means squishing cucumber beetles, picking off slugs and feeding them to chickens, and capturing mice, moles, and gophers with traps.

Then there's the more conventional method, but it doesn't work particularly well for a backyard garden, not to mention for people who eat vegetables or are concerned with how their actions affect their souls. This method involves spraying a field with broad-spectrum pesticides that kill bees along with cucumber beetles, ladybugs along with aphids, and butterflies besides. It kills what is beautiful, useful, and necessary for pollination along with what is destructive and damaging. It fails to see our interconnection with other living things and our place within creation.

Even if humans didn't need bees and other pollinators to have access to certain fruits and vegetables, bees exist because God wants them to exist. God gives them life and a place in the world with a task to do, which they do simply by living out their creaturely lives and basking in the pleasure of doing so.

Furthermore, why would any of us feed our children (or feed ourselves) food sprayed with a poison that is potent enough to kill, especially when it comes with labels that warn users to keep children and pets away and to use breathing masks, gloves, and protective rubber clothing during application? Can we just wash that poison off our lettuce and not think the leaves have absorbed it into their watery cells like rain from the sky?

Being in a garden changes your relationship to the land if you let it. We find ourselves noticing, appreciating, and standing in awe of its intricacies, of the relationships that work together to produce fruit and feed ladybugs, garden spiders, worms, and microbes.

The garden is a hope-filled place. By working tenaciously, seeing a place in its entirety, and recognizing one's role and need to fit into a bigger, wilder, and older whole, a respect for place can begin to take root.

I've wondered whether our failure to be good gardeners—that is, tenacious and hopeful stewards of creation—might thwart our development, particularly as members that belong to the whole of God's earth. If we can't see ourselves as part of creation, does it make it easier for us to collectively exploit the land, harm and abuse its creatures in an assortment of ways, and mistreat other people who also depend on the land to flourish?

This question quickly becomes overwhelming. Sometimes I need to take a break from the questions and simply don my gloves, grab my small hand hoe, and go weed the herb garden or the flower beds. This simple work grounds me. When I am finished, my beds are neat and my soul, more often than not, is calmer, more centered, and refreshed. I cannot explain why it works this way, except perhaps that weeding is good work, and good work is a balm for the soul. Weeding requires only that I be tenacious and hold on to the hope that a cared-for garden can flourish.

I suppose we hoe and pick off slugs because the hope of things that we envision and long for is, in fact, a fairly good gamble. The seasons offer enough predictability that we can usually count on good-enough outcomes for our efforts. That energy-inspiring hope has kept humanity planting, cultivating, hoeing, and attending to various pests generation after generation.

Good Thing #6: We Learn That Some Stress Is Good

A coddled plant does not grow strong. Then again, neither does a neglected one.

Plants, bones, and people need stress to grow strong—not too much but also not too little. To be able to withstand storms and drought and nibbling by hungry creatures, plants need deep roots underground and healthy foliage above it. Plants grow deep roots when the water they receive is adequate but somewhat infrequent (once or twice a week). Infrequent watering stresses a plant enough to incline it to send roots downward into the moist soil, which is a reservoir of sorts, a place of life-giving water. When plants are watered a little bit every day, their roots hang around near the surface of the soil. As a result, they crumple up and wilt during the first heat wave because that little bit of daily water inadequately prepared them for the tribulation of a hot week.

We prune trees and fruit-bearing shrubs to clear out the clutter and let the light in. Light needs to access the inner parts of trees for them to develop well. Pruning also grows branches strong so they can bear much fruit. When they are young, trees seem enthusiastic about putting out blossoms, as if they want to show what they are capable of before they are actually capable of it. The bees fertilize the trees' blossoms, and little limbs try to bear a load of fruit they are ill-prepared to carry. We've lost big limbs off peach and apple trees that way and have learned not only to prune branches but also to thin fruit, removing a third to half of it, even after the trees have matured. While pruning involves a certain amount of stress for the tree, *not* pruning can leave the trees weak and vulnerable to breaking.

Stress (not too much, not too little) is good for gardeners too. If we never have problems with pests or invasive weeds, if we never experience cold snaps or heat waves, how will we gain any confidence that we can handle the inevitable challenges when they come? If we always avoid working in the rain, in the cold, or in 100-degree weather, what opportunities are we missing for learning what our bodies can do and what makes it possible for them to function adequately in extreme and uncomfortable circumstances?

In 2003 Aron Ralston went backpacking alone in the Blue John Canyon and got his hand and wrist trapped under a boulder in a canyoneering accident. Since no one knew where he had gone or even *that* he had gone, he didn't expect anyone to come looking for him. Ralston had two choices: try to free his arm or give up and die. He wanted to live, so he spent the first three days sipping water and trying to break, chip, and move the boulder that trapped him. On day four he ran out of water and realized he'd have to leave his forearm behind. I'll spare you the details, but it took him a while. Ralston managed to amputate his forearm and climb out of the canyon. He lived. The moral of the story—as I told it to my daughter, who wanted to take a solo backpacking trip—is "Don't go backpacking alone."

In response she said, "No, Mom, the moral of the story is that humans have the capacity to do what it takes to survive when they have to."

We were both right. Aron would not have been able to save himself if he had not previously faced significant and stressful challenges and misadventures.

Stress strengthens. Is it too bold an assertion to say that stress saves us? As we practice responding well and learning from stress, we gain confidence and skills that prepare us for the bigger challenges to come. In our weakness we can be made strong. God assures us of that, and the apostle Paul affirms it in both 2 Corinthians 12 and in Romans 5:3–5, where he writes: "We can rejoice, too, when we run into problems and trials, for we know that they help us develop endurance. And endurance develops strength of character, and character strengthens our confident hope of salvation. And this hope will not lead to disappointment. For we know how dearly God loves us, because he has given us the Holy Spirit to fill our hearts with his love."

The trick for a plant, a bone, a person, or a marriage is figuring out how much stress is enough. We slow down our watering of tomatoes to stress the plant into producing fruit and to keep the fruit from ballooning up with water and losing flavor. But if tomato plants don't have enough calcium, which they get from the soil, the tomatoes develop bottom rot; and the best way to fix *that* is to water them so they can draw the calcium into their growing bodies.

Watering can be tricky business.

A bone needs some impact to stay strong, but too much running or dancing or marching and one gets shin splints. A certain amount of stress keeps a person or a marriage attentive and alert, but too much can cause it to flounder.

As a sociologist, I join a good number of my colleagues in thinking that Western culture avoids stress. We overprotect our children to prevent them from ever making bad choices. To keep them from emotional pain or danger, we shield them from disappointment or the possibility of falling out of a tree. To boost their self-esteem, we tell them that everything they make is beautiful and that they are smart, unique, and special. Sociologists studying families have a growing concern that we are raising a generation with little resilience to life's challenges.

One of my students told me that she learned she was not particularly unique or special or amazingly smart when she got to college. She had internalized these ideas growing up, having heard them repeatedly from adults in her life. In college she realized that everyone around her had grown up hearing that they were unique and special, which made her wonder what it means to be special since *everyone* apparently is. She's handled a fair amount of pain and stress in the last few years and has told me that growing up in a relatively stress- and danger-free environment didn't prepare her for the hard times that came.

Hard times always come.

Depending on Advil, Ambien, beer, wine, television, or the internet to cope with stress, pain, and sleeplessness doesn't help us learn what we are capable of, nor does it help us find the strength that comes from living through a hard thing, accepting reality, and finding some way to embrace it, grow strong from it, and experience God with us in it. What could it look like for small groups or church communities to own this as a responsibility so that we can help each other live well through hard times?

That's not to say I don't take Advil occasionally for muscle pain or a headache. But sometimes when our heads hurt, maybe what we need more than Advil is water, more sleep, some time outside in our natural habitat, and some time alone. Maybe we also need the humility and the courage to set aside our tyrannical to-do list and realize the world will go on even if we don't get everything on our list accomplished. Maybe we need a Sabbath rest.

Might leaning into stress and paying attention to its pains root us more deeply in God's life-sustaining love? I don't intend for gardening to simply be a metaphor. Observing and working as a steward of the land can help us learn that stress is part of life and that various parts cooperate and compete. Daily stress in the garden and outside the garden offers practice grounds for developing endurance, strength of character, and hope.

Mark and I learn that with persistence and a bit of troubleshooting we can eventually get beans to sprout, and we learn to accept that raccoons will occasionally cause mischief at inopportune times. Experiences such as these offer opportunities to practice living fearlessly and to not let outward failure dishearten or take away joy but open the eyes of our souls to see good in all things.

Good Thing #7: We Learn to Pay Attention

I have a confession to make. When I used to walk by older folks working in their vegetable or flower gardens, I thought they were "cute"—that is to say, quaint, and not to be taken seriously. I thought, *Good for those retired folks with so little work to do! Good for them that they are choosing to be outside puttering around in their little yards rather than inside watching television.*

The closer in age I get to those older folks, the more I wonder whether maybe growing older helps one see the falseness in a life lived too much inside buildings doing this or that seemingly important thing and forgetting all the life that's lived outside those walls in forests, under the ground, and in the sky. Maybe those older folks in their gardens see the shallowness associated with things born inside buildings more clearly—things like fashion, notions of the perfect body, and the need to acquire stuff and stamps on one's passports from places like the Bahamas or France.

I've read from and heard old souls speak about figuring out that years spent striving for status and advancement don't matter as much as humbly accepting one's small role in some greater story. At the end of the day, these wise friends have lived toward a good relationship with God, with others, and with the natural world more than for job advancement, accolades, or positions of honor.

"Pay attention. / Be astonished. / Tell about it," says Mary Oliver, who has spent her life writing poetry that does just that.[7] When we pay attention we might find ourselves humbly astonished by the beauty, the complementarity, the fragility, and the strength of the world. We might see how life on earth reproduces itself and is sustained by fairly predictable cycles that bring the necessary ingredients together so that apple blossoms become fruit and beans dried by the sun become protein-rich pebbles of goodness that can fill hungry stomachs on winter nights.

Working in a garden calls one to attention.

So there you have it, seven good things that can come from gardening. Almost anyone can grow a tomato plant on a patio or some herbs in the window. Anyone can choose to watch the wonder of a seed transformed from a single dry bean in the hand to a vine that grows ten feet up the side of a bean teepee, producing a bucket of beans, each of which holds six or seven individual seeds. Not all that much is required to grow food. Food happens. Growing it might connect us to practices and principles that we easily forget when someone else far away and invisible to us grows our food.

The closer we are to the growing and harvesting of food, the more we can understand the sacrifice and labor associated with growing and harvesting. I imagine that the closer we are to growing food, the less likely we are to take the daily grace of food for granted.

The Fern Creek Market overflows with goodness in late August, which is the midpoint in our season. Along one wall sits the canning kettle filled with bundles of kale, collards, and chard. The kettle shares that shelf with crates full of zucchini, yellow squash, crookneck and tromboncino squash, onions and eggplant, beets, broccoli, and potatoes. On the back wall are a variety of red and colorful heirloom tomatoes, Honeycrisp apples, green beans, corn, and cucumbers. The final shelf—the "Pick Two" shelf—holds fennel and kohlrabi, green and purple cabbage, baby potatoes, rhubarb, patty pan squash, and more greens. In the "Help Yourself" crate and basket are oversized summer squash, little onions that won't keep through the winter, and windfall apples. All of this abundance comes as a gift from the gardens, from the soil, water, and sun.

After we have completed the harvest on Mondays and Thursdays, set up the market, and swept the floor, the four of us stand there a minute. Sometimes we stand together, but more often just one or two of us stand at a time. We marvel in our own ways at the bounty and beauty we have hauled in from the fields. How is it that all of this food grew in so short a time? How did the fields that looked relatively bare just two months ago produce such bounty?

One afternoon over lunch we decided that our moment of awe and appreciation was a moment of worship—a Sabbath moment in which there was nowhere else we wanted to be and nothing else we needed or wanted to be doing. Our only desire was to stand and savor our work. However crazy it sounds, at such moments I experience a mystical community that includes not only the people who work alongside me but also the soil, plants, nonhuman laborers, and human and nonhuman eaters who come together at Fern Creek.

• *Roasted Summer Vegetables* •
(Fennel, Broccoli, Summer Squash)

Eat roasted vegetables as a side dish, top a pizza with them, or add them to a pasta dish, salad, or omelet. Roasted vegetables are versatile and equally wonderful on the second, third, and fourth days.

I prefer roasting vegetables in medleys of two or three, which allows the flavors not only to blend but also to stand out without getting lost in the shuffle of too many vegetables. Many vegetables lend themselves to roasting. Alternative combinations to the recipe below include: beets, carrots, and winter squash (delicata is a great roasting squash); yams, potatoes, and onions; baby red, new, or fingerling potatoes and rosemary; and kale and sea salt.

Preheat the oven to 400 degrees.

Thinly slice fennel (or onions) and place on a baking tray in a single layer. Drizzle with olive oil and roast for 10 minutes to give them a head start toward caramelizing.

Meanwhile, slice summer squash (tromboncino is excellent) and cut broccoli into florets. Add to the onions, drizzle with more olive oil, and sprinkle with sea salt. Optional: add herbs like rosemary, basil, and oregano.

Roast another 10–15 minutes or until the squash is tender and the broccoli is browning on the edges.

When roasting vegetables that require more time, stir occasionally. The harder and denser the raw vegetable is, the longer it will take to roast. Beets take the longest of all—an hour or more. Wrap beets in foil and roast them in their own pan, giving them a head start on whatever else you're roasting. Quarter or halve them to speed up roasting time. In all cases, the smaller you chop the pieces, the quicker they roast.

Reflections and Questions

1. What kinds of weeds need to be hoed in your life to allow you to flourish? What habits, beliefs, and practices keep you from being more fully who you are created to be?

2. We all make mistakes, and all mistakes have been made before we made them. Which of life's big mistakes did you avoid, and what helped you avoid them? Which ones did you make, and looking back, how might they have been avoided? Where has God's grace (perhaps mediated through others) both *saved* you from making the worst mistakes and *helped* you find your way forward in the midst of having made mistakes, even the worst ones?

3. Can you think of a time when you chose the harder but better path to deal with a life difficulty? Can you also think of a time you chose an easier path, one that ultimately did more harm than good? What helps make it possible to choose the harder but perhaps better path for dealing with life difficulties?

4. The chapter says that "work is good when it recognizes and honors our dependence on the earth, fosters collaborative relationships with other members of creation, uses our God-given creativity, and grants us freedom to choose how we work and what we do with the fruits of our labors." The opposite kind of work alienates us from creation, others, our own creativity, and sometimes our conscience. You have probably done work that falls into both of these categories and work that seemingly falls into neither. Would it help people going back to work, choosing careers, and contemplating changing jobs to have conversations about meaningful work within their faith communities? If so, how might you help initiate part of that conversation in your sphere of influence?

5. Reflect or talk about the balance of wanting to do good work that acknowledges we belong to a particular place and community with a desire to do good work and pursue opportunities that take us elsewhere. What have your choices been in this regard? What would you do differently, and what would you repeat?

6. The chapter says that some stress for plants (and people) is good—not too much but also not too little. It then critiques our culture as being stress avoidant, depending too much on aids like Ambien, wine, and the internet to deal with stress, pain, and sleeplessness. In doing so we are losing the opportunity to "find the strength that comes from living through a hard thing, accepting reality, and finding some way to embrace it, grow strong from it, and experience

God with us in it." What about this critique resonates with you or challenges you?

7. What has practicing and honoring the Sabbath looked like for you over the course of your life? Has it ever been an intentional practice? What was that like, and if you used to practice it more intentionally than you do now, why do you think you stopped?

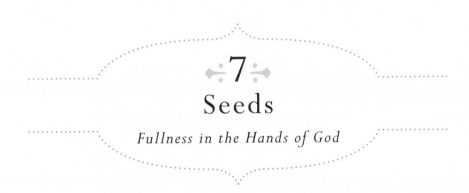

7

Seeds

Fullness in the Hands of God

I want to tell you about the most hopeful thing in the world. It is a seed.

—Janisse Ray[1]

In the beginning God spoke, and a universe that was not came into being. Light emerged out of darkness, and matter out of a void of nothingness.

God cast a seed, as it were, into that dark nothingness. A seed containing the power of all that was, and is, and will be possible—all that would be needed for galaxies, suns, planets, moons, and life as we know it to exist on this tiny fleck in the Virgo Supercluster of galaxies.

God created, as we earthlings are wont to say, with Earth in mind. We live on the third planet from our Sun in a group of eight planets, numerous comets and asteroids, and what we now call "dwarf planets" that orbit the Sun. Our little solar system is in the Orion Arm, a spiral arm of the Milky Way. The Milky Way, *our* Milky Way (as we are also inclined to say), is a large spiral of stars that we can see straight above our heads on moonless nights—that is, if one is lucky enough to live away from city lights that are meant to hold back the night's darkness. It is the second largest galaxy in one local group of galaxies in the Virgo Supercluster, itself only one supercluster of many in the knowable universe. In the big scheme of things, we are small, which does not change my belief that God had us in mind in the beginning.

God created a universe that would come into its fullness, infusing all that was needed with the spoken Word, with a seed that is coming into fullness yet. If the universe is still expanding, might that also mean that the fullness of earth is yet to be realized, yet to be complete in every particular way, to become all that is possible?

If one imagines creation beginning with a seed that God planted, then a large pumpkin seed or a tiny carrot seed is more than a metaphor. It is God at work, still.

That's why I want to feel that I am holding something miraculous when I cup seeds in my hand. I want to treat them as something sacred, the power of God at work. I struggle with this because seeds are so ordinary. They are everywhere: on dandelions that have become balls of fluff, in bean pods, on ears of corn, inside apples and plums, and at the tips of each rubbery leek strand making beautiful softball-size purple balls that leeks send forth when they "go to seed," we say, as though it's a bad thing.

Some seeds we save for the next year's planting. We eat some, feed some to the chickens, and compost many. A miracle is supposed to be something that defies the laws of nature, like being raised from the dead. Miracles are surprising and positive events that can't be explained and so are attributed to the work of a divine being. I realize seeds are not truly miraculous, even if seeds *do* rise from the dead every spring. A sprouting seed is not surprising, and science explains it adequately. Maybe we need another word for ordinary processes that do extraordinary things at the pleasure and will of a divine being. Or maybe we just need to reclaim the good of the word *ordinary*.

Brief (but relevant) detour: I'm writing in the tree house, and an entirely yellow spider the size of a ladybug just dropped herself onto my computer. She is neon yellow, almost fluorescent. I watch her make her way back up to the safety of the tree branch from which she came wafting down. Then I take a mental pause from writing to research her, and I discover that we call such spiders goldenrod crab spiders, which seems like a pretty good description. Hmm . . . what do dung beetles and ladybugs, aphids and crab spiders, oak and birch trees, pumpkins, carrots, pigs, and people have in common? They come from a seed. There are a lot of different life forms on the earth—a *lot*—which is a good thing, it turns out. Seeds make life possible, keeping a fairly predictable flow of life going from one generation to the next.

Maybe a proper response to running my finger over knobby beet seeds, round peas, or itsy-bitsy lettuce seeds in the palm of my hand is to praise God for crafting a world so full of reliable predictability and diversity. Seeds are that seemingly inconsequential bit of grit or flake or pebble that determines a thing's biological destiny. We come from seed, and all life moves forward because of seed.

As God's caretakers of the garden, we are keepers of seeds. Controversy, politics, and economic questions surround the keeping, modifying, buying, and selling of seeds. Might one outward expression of our charge to be stewards of the food supply be seed keeping?

About Seeds

Hybrid. Heirloom. Genetically modified. Seed saving. Food sovereignty. These terms pop up in conversations about seeds, spoken as though everyone understands their meanings. I created a glossary of terms (you'll find it later in this chapter), partly because *I* needed clarification to better understand and talk about questions like "What's the problem with genetically modified seeds?" and "Why should conversations about seeds be important to me, and what can I do as a non-gardener or limited gardener?"

Here are three biological facts that may or may not seem obvious. First, the health of life depends on the reproduction of a wide variety of species—animals as well as plants. It's obvious that life depends on reproduction; what may seem less obvious is why a wide variety of plant and animal species need to keep reproducing to keep any particular species alive and well. Back to that in a moment.

Second, every organism, as a group, produces more offspring than will survive to adulthood. While all offspring have unique characteristics, only those that make it to adulthood and manage to reproduce pass characteristics on to the next generation. The survivors (and now I'm speaking of plants) are the ones with traits that help them better withstand drought or freezing temperatures or have taller or shorter stalks—depending on which one survived long enough to reproduce within the troubles and travails of their given environment.

Third, a good bit of variation occurs over time as plant species adapt and change to thrive in particular climates and environments. That diversity is a great life insurance policy for all animals that eat plants, as well as for plants that need animals to eat their fruit for them to thrive. (Think of the cherry that gets eaten by a bird: the seed is transported and then dropped rather unceremoniously from the sky onto a new spot of soil where it has a chance to grow strong without having to compete with hundreds of other cherry saplings sprouting under the mama tree.)

Some seeds have developed to survive drought better, while other seeds produce more peas in every pod or grains on every stalk. Other variants

⊹ *A Glossary of Terms* ⊹

biodiversity. The amount of variation of life in a specified area, such as a backyard garden, a 50,000-acre farm, a rain forest, or the entire earth. Variation ensures a large, strong genetic pool. A farm made up only of corn or chickens is more susceptible to failure than a farm with diverse crops and animals. If hail takes out the corn, the diverse farmer still has potatoes, strawberries, eggs from the chickens, and milk from the cows.

  biotechnology. The use of biological processes, cells, bacteria, etc., for industrial purposes, especially the genetic manipulation of microorganisms on a cellular level to affect outcomes.

  food sovereignty. The right of people to healthy and culturally appropriate food that is produced in ecologically sound and sustainable ways; people's right to determine their own food systems.[2] This began as an indigenous people's movement in the Global South and has moved north- and westward.

  genetically modified. When a crop (or any organism) has been artificially altered (its DNA changed) to achieve some desired characteristic that would not otherwise occur. This process uses what the industry refers to as transgenic technology. GMO stands for genetically modified organism. GM corn or GM soy is how the seed is typically referred to. GE (genetically engineered) and biotech crops are synonyms.

  heirloom. A variety that has been around a long time (at least fifty years, although many have been around hundreds or thousands of years), passing down stable traits from one generation to the next. Heirloom seeds can be saved and replanted from year to year. They are open-pollinated, that is, pollinated by insects, birds, or the wind, which makes them more genetically diverse and allows them to slowly adapt to changes in climate or pests over the years. Because heirlooms tend to be less predictable in size and shape and don't ship well or keep as long or become ripe at the same time (which makes large-scale harvesting easier), they have been largely replaced by hybrids. The Gravenstein apple, for example, tastes divinely tart and sweet. However, the apples ripen over a long period of time rather than in a short harvesting window, they bruise easily, and the trees are more, well, *sensitive*. As a result, they have become an uncommon apple in the industry.

hybrid. The offspring of two different plant varieties interbred so that their offspring have characteristics of both. Cross-pollination is a natural process, but creating hybrids is a carefully controlled breeding program. Seeds from hybrids will not reproduce "true" in the next season, so these seeds cannot be saved and planted the next year, at least not with confidence of replicating what was initially planted. The Honeycrisp apple is a hybrid of Macoun and Honeygold apples, deliciously sweet, fairly predictable in size and shape, and with a tendency to mature on the tree at roughly the same time.

Monsanto. The largest multinational agrochemical and agricultural biotechnology corporation, headquartered in Missouri. Monsanto is the biggest seller of GM seeds on the global market (90 percent of soy, 95 percent of corn). They also produce and sell Roundup, a common herbicide, which is used with seed that has been genetically modified so that it won't die when Roundup is sprayed on a field to rid it of weeds.

organic. Most simply it means food grown or raised without the use of synthetic chemicals. Certified Organic is a label used by growers subscribing to a set protocol that ensures crops are not treated with synthetic fertilizers, herbicides, and pesticides. By definition something cannot be labeled organic and come from genetically modified seed. The process is heavily regulated and requires extensive record keeping and accountability. Small growers unable to afford the certification but still committed to growing organically use terms like "naturally grown," a label that can be abused. Farmers who grow their crops organically but are not certified attempt to fully disclose their farming and ranching practices and use supplies approved by the Organic Materials Review Institute (OMRI).[3]

seed patents. A patent grants the exclusive right to the "inventor" to make and sell a particular product, making it illegal to save or exchange patented seeds. Patents allow corporations to sue farmers who grow unpurchased patented seed in their fields. Initially, patents were used only for the development of new hybrids, but now they extend to centuries-old seed. For instance, basmati rice, which has been cultivated in the Indian subcontinent for centuries, was successfully patented in 1997. Seed patents are perceived as the number one threat to food sovereignty, creating dependence on multinational corporations (like Monsanto) for seeds. Since seeds are not inventions (even GM seed depends on preexisting seeds), groups fighting for food sovereignty perceive patents as illegitimate, a form of *biopiracy* (the exploitation and monopolizing of naturally occurring biological or genetic material).

seed saving. A global and historical practice of keeping and exchanging heirloom and other open-pollinated seeds from one year to the next, keeping seed diversity alive and well. This practice is illegal for patented seed.

survive hot summers or cold winters better than those that have adapted to survive the nibbling of pests. The earth maintains a spectrum of diverse traits so that when catastrophes come, genetic diversity ensures that a stable food supply will still be around once the dust settles.

Then humans started tinkering with the process, because tinkering is what humans do. As stewards—creators made in the image of God—we tinker, for good and for ill. Long ago, humans observed the natural selection process in plants and animals and have crossbred both for several thousand years. The process moved to the laboratory after plant breeder Gregor Mendel published a scientific paper in 1865 about using artificial fertilizations to create hybrids. The paper was largely ignored until the 1900s, but now his ideas are so highly regarded that Mendel is considered the father of genetics. In the 1920s researchers started experimenting with the X-ray to try to induce (that is, speed up) a mutation process that might typically take hundreds or thousands of years to occur naturally. After WWII, an assortment of chemicals and gamma rays, protons, neutrons, alpha particles, and beta particles (which all became possible in the nuclear age) were thrown at seeds in an attempt to induce mutations. Not that it was as haphazard as that sounds. In the 1970s DNA cloning allowed genes from one organism to be implanted in another, and by the 1980s transgenic technology made it possible for a gene from a fairly distant organism to be transplanted in another (such as a bacteria into corn).[4]

Monsanto scientists were among the first to genetically modify a plant cell. The first widespread purchasing of genetically modified seed was in the mid-1990s, as technology continued to push back the limits of what commercial growers could do. Crops (like Roundup Ready soybeans and corn) could be altered to resist herbicides or formulated with built-in pesticide (like Bt, a toxic bacteria that kills corn-eating caterpillars).

The use of transgenic technology to create genetically modified (GM) seed exploded in the late 1990s. By 2000, 17 percent of corn grown in the United States was genetically modified, as well as 43 percent of soybeans. According to 2014 USDA records, 99 percent of soybeans, 91 percent of corn, and 98 percent of cotton grown in the United States was genetically modified.[5] (Cottonseed oil is a primary ingredient in Crisco and other vegetable shortenings and, being inexpensive, is used in a wide range of processed foods.)

That's a brief history of how we got where we are. The controversy surrounding genetically modified seed, and therefore food, is strong. I'll summarize the reasons given in support of GM seeds, but up front let me say (in case you haven't guessed already) that I'm biased. I'm a GMO (genetically modified organism) naysayer, which is a position that needs to be heard more often than it is. Later in this chapter, I'll spend some time arguing against the use of GMOs.

The Promising Side of GM Seeds

The effort to get more food out of every acre began altruistically. Combine the need for more food with the curiosity of humans to tinker, create, and manipulate variables and elements, and you've got the perfect brew for invention. Biologists already understood breeding and were gaining knowledge about how to manipulate genes in animals and plants to get desired outcomes, such as increased size and quantity or resistance to drought. Even if the motives were mixed (there is always money to be made), more food out of every acre helped to feed a human population that was exploding both domestically and abroad. Crop yield goes up with GM crops, especially with corn. GM seed can have increased resistance to drought, pests, and weeds, all of which can help feed hungry people when food shortages loom. That's no small thing if you live in China, India, or various countries in Africa where access to food has been tenuous because of political instability, drought, land degradation, soil erosion, and perhaps most of all, trade policies that undermine African agriculture. In all of these countries GM seed has been introduced as a possible solution to food shortages.

In addition, GM crops altered with Bt (*bacillus thuringiensis*—a bacteria spliced into most GM corn, soy, and cotton to kill various pests) require less pesticide spray. Less pesticide spray (which is typically used in conventional farming) means that beneficial insects are alive to eat other plant-eating insects not killed by the Bt toxin, like aphids. So GM seed with Bt may be a better choice for the environment than farming with conventional pesticides that tend to be sprayed liberally, killing pests and pollinators alike.[6] Less pesticide use is better for the other living organisms in the area, better for field laborers (who are exposed to fewer toxins), and possibly better for people who eat the produce. The jury is out regarding the potential health impact of eating crops spliced with Bt compared to those heavily sprayed with pesticides. It is worth noting that Bt is a naturally occurring bacteria and an active ingredient in various products approved by the Organic Materials Review Institute (OMRI). However, Bt can be genetically modified, and any strain or subsequent product (like Bt corn) that has been genetically modified is not OMRI approved.

Using GM seeds can save farmers money since they spend less on pesticides and labor for weeding and because they get a greater yield for the investment of their time and money. Given the lack of clear evidence regarding the safety of consuming GM seed and foods made from GM crops, the supporters of GMOs say that the benefits far outweigh the liabilities.

The Dark Side of the GMO Story

Those who oppose GMOs want to tell a bigger story.

Less than a century after serious plant breeding started, US agricultural land is peppered with genetically uniform crops. Commercially, only a few varieties of corn are planted anymore, and the same is true for soybeans and wheat. Since GM seeds give fairly predictable high yields, conventional farmers feel fiscally foolish not to plant the highest-yielding variety.

The result is that we have a shallow gene bank in the United States, which makes us vulnerable to the unexpected—such as a superpest that emerges and takes out a whole variety of corn; or the rootworm, which has now developed a resistance to Bt; or an especially hot, wet, or cold season. Thankfully, diversity still exists, primarily in the Global South. So it's okay if we experiment with our agricultural practices so long as those folks south of us keep the global seed bank safe. Without being explicit about it, we rely on seed savers in the Global South in case something comes along and wipes out our few high-producing varieties of corn, wheat, or soy. Barbara Kingsolver and Janisse Ray in the United States, Vandana Shiva from India, and environmental activists and writers across Africa argue that we are now engaged in an effort to cancel that insurance; when farmers and countries lose control of their seeds by adopting GM seeds, they lose both food security and food sovereignty.

Here's a scenario Kingsolver offers in her essay "Fist in the Eye of God."

Let's say you are an Ethiopian farmer growing a land race of wheat—a wildly variable, husky mongrel crop that has been in your family for hundreds of years. You always lose some to wind and weather, but the rest still comes through every year. Lately, though, you've been hearing about a kind of Magic Wheat that grows six times bigger than your crop, is easier to harvest, and contains vitamins that aren't found in ordinary wheat. And amazingly enough, by special arrangement with the government, it's free.

Readers who have even the slightest acquaintance with fairy tales will already know there is trouble ahead in this story. The Magic Wheat grows well the first year, but its rapid, overly green growth attracts a startling number of pests. You see insects on this crop that never ate wheat before, in the whole of your family's history. You watch, you worry. You realize that you're going to have to spray a pesticide to get this crop through to harvest. You're not so surprised to learn that by special arrangement with the government, the same company that gave you the seed for free can sell you the pesticide you need. It's a good pesticide, they use it all the time in America, but it costs money you don't have, so you'll have to borrow against next year's crop.

The second year, you will be visited by a terrible drought, and your crop will not survive to harvest at all; every stalk dies. Magic Wheat from America doesn't know beans about Ethiopian drought. The end.

   Actually, if the drought arrived in year two and the end came that quickly, in this real-life fairy tale you'd be very lucky, because chances are good you'd still have some of your family-line seed around. It would be much more disastrous if the drought waited until the eighth or ninth year to wipe you out, for then you'd have no wheat left at all, Magic or otherwise. Seed banks, even if they're eleven thousand years old, can't survive for more than a few years on the shelf. If they aren't grown out as crops year after year, they die—or else get ground into flour and baked and eaten—and then this product of a thousand hands and careful selection is just gone, once and for all.[7]

Neither genetically modified crops nor the many hybrids that are now manufactured can have the resilience of seed that is tried and reproduced naturally under the varying conditions of rain, drought, pests, and temperature extremes.

While it's true that GM crops have lessened the amount of pesticides used, more herbicides are being applied since a number of crops are now Roundup Ready. Besides devastating soil health by purging the soil of necessary plant matter that feeds and nourishes it, sprayed herbicides float to neighboring farms, killing crops, ground cover, and plants that have not been genetically modified to withstand Roundup.

And if all that evidence doesn't give one pause, perhaps the fact that nature is fighting back will. Weeds have adapted to their hard circumstances, as all living beings tend to do (thank God), and "superweeds" that have grown resistant to Roundup now compete with Roundup Ready seed crops for space and soil nutrients. Likewise, superpests such as corn rootworm have developed a resistance to Bt corn and no longer die when they eat it. That has created a problem on a whole different scale.

Loss of food sovereignty and the compromise of the ecological health of agricultural lands are two primary reasons for opposing GMOs, but the one that has most captured the attention of people in the United States is the unknown effects of eating GM foods. We are consuming food made from crops embedded with a toxin that kills pests. These crops are then raised in a sea of herbicides that contain poisons the crops themselves have been bred to resist. I sometimes wonder if Bt corn would technically qualify as a pesticide. If so, wouldn't that mean that when people eat foods with Bt corn or soy, they are eating pesticides drenched in herbicides? How could that *not* negatively affect our health?

GM wheat has not yet been legally approved anywhere in the world. As of 2014 Monsanto said they are just a few years out from having it commercially available. While it's easy to confuse GM crops with hybrids, they are not the same thing (see the glossary). Still, some hybrids are proving problematic. Let's consider hybridized wheat. It became readily available in the 1990s, and in the last twenty-five years we've seen a corresponding rise in celiac disease and gluten intolerance. Research is suggesting that the higher concentration of gluten proteins in hybrid wheat may be contributing to the increase of celiac disease and gluten intolerances.[8] It makes sense that, collectively, the human gut would take generations to adapt to modifications that generally take place over centuries in the natural world. That our bodies have physical trouble adapting (over the course of a decade) to food changed in laboratories doesn't surprise medical researchers, nutritionists, and the likes of cardiologist William David, author of the popular book *Wheat Belly: Lose the Wheat, Lose the Weight and Find Your Path Back to Health*.

Studies about health and GMOs are somewhat inconclusive but suggest links between GM foods and food allergies, cancers, obesity, anxiety disorders, and the increase of autism and other behavioral problems in children. Jeffrey Smith was an executive with the leading independent laboratory that tests food for the presence of GM crops. He's one of the primary spokespeople for the health dangers of GM foods and the power of corporate influence to cover up or minimize the risks. He has written numerous articles, and his book *Seeds of Deception: Exposing Industry and Government Lies about the Safety of the Genetically Engineered Foods You're Eating* is frequently cited by those ringing alarm bells about the affects of GM food on health.

The American Academy of Environmental Medicine (AAEM) recommends that the United States put a moratorium on GM foods and that physicians educate their patients about the potential risks of eating them. The article summarizes studies of animals fed GM diets and says mounting evidence shows links to an assortment of organ problems. Livers deteriorated, and cardio, pancreatic, kidney, reproductive, and intestinal systems were negatively affected.[9]

Yet GMO Answers (at gmoanswers.com) claims that nearly twenty years of animal research shows GM foods to be safe and to have no significant impact on the health of animals. Their conclusion is that GM foods are therefore safe for people to consume. GMO Answers also reports that the American Academy of Environmental Medicine is a questionable organization. So I went hunting and found that the AAEM is accredited to provide the continuing medical education required of all physicians, even though it is not listed as one of the American Medical Association's (AMA) specialty societies. In 2012 the AMA also supported requiring premarket testing for the safety of all GM foods. When I researched who funds GMO Answers, which is an initiative of the Council for Biotechnology Information, I discovered that the contributors include Monsanto, Syngenta, Dow AgroSciences, DuPont, and Bayer CropScience—all large producers of GM seed.

There is still much unknown about the health impacts of eating GM foods. Personally, I don't need to be compelled by the health argument because I'm convinced by the bigger picture. Part of that convincing comes from learning how the world has responded to the availability of GM seeds.

Listening In at the Global Table

In our best moments, don't we all seek outside perspectives to help us figure out how we should think and feel about a thing? I find it comforting to think that better answers can be found in a community rather than believing I have to determine them on my own, but that means being willing to go outside my typical sources. There is a substantial pool of knowledge and wisdom outside the United States that is maintained by cultures much older than ours. These people have been seeking to craft good and meaningful lives for many more generations than we have and have seen the world change over millennia rather than just a few centuries.

Since seeds have been with us since the beginning, I wanted to know what the rest of the world thought of genetically modified seed as a way to address world hunger. This is what I learned.

The European Union is not a huge fan. In fact, they are not fans at all. The EU has the most stringent labeling requirements for GM foods and strict regulations on the importing and use of GM seeds. A few EU countries (such as Spain) allow some GM crops, but most of them do not.

The African Union declared 2014 the Year of Food Security and has a goal of eradicating hunger in Africa by 2025. Some think GM seeds will help them get there; others are pretty sure they will not and are fighting to keep GM seeds (and Monsanto) out. In October 2013, seven African countries joined together in a "March against Monsanto," and as of 2014 only Egypt, South Africa, Sudan, and Burkina Faso allow GM seed into their countries. The issue for some African leaders is transferring ownership of seeds from farmers to big corporations like Monsanto. They are fairly certain that food security is impossible without control of one's seed supply. Perhaps that inclination comes from experiencing the kinds of devastation that result from political unrest and corruption from within and exploitation and colonization from without. A number of African countries also reject food aid that comes in the form of GM seeds.

India has been embroiled in controversy over GM seed, out of which emerged perhaps the largest activist group fighting on behalf of seeds. From the late 1990s until 2010, GM seed was increasingly being bought and planted in India as part of a plan to feed the masses in order to prevent the kinds of deaths that happened with the Bengal famine in 1943, which killed two million Indians. By 2010 India's protest against GM seed was strong enough to get the government to put a moratorium on the importing and use of GM seeds. As of 2014 the ban on GM seed for food crops continues, although GM cotton is widely planted across India.[10]

GM seeds continue to be most welcome in the United States, China, Argentina, Brazil, and Australia. It gives me pause when I realize that most of the world isn't buying into the GM seed quite so readily as we have. Neither do they have as many lobbyists in agribusiness working to keep states from passing legislation that requires them to identify food products using GM seed.

Indian environmental activist Vandana Shiva is an antiglobalization (or prolocalization) advocate and author. She has a PhD in philosophy and has authored more than twenty books on related topics. She argues for a return to and respect for the wisdom of traditional practices rooted in local communities. Much of her work centers on the practice of agriculture and food, but she also researches biodiversity, bioethics, and genetic engineering.

Navdanya ("nine seeds") is a network of seed keepers, organic farmers, and food producers that is active in seventeen of India's twenty-nine states. In the last twenty years, the Navdanya network has helped set up 111 community seed banks and trained over half a million farmers in seed sovereignty, food sovereignty, and sustainable agriculture. Navdanya is the largest direct-marketing, fair-trade organic network in India, which is the second most populated country in the world—just behind China. Much that is good is happening in India, good that serves the whole world well.[11]

There's some active fighting on behalf of food sovereignty in South and Central America and Mexico as well. La Via Campesina is a group that advocates for culturally appropriate, ecologically sound (no GMOs), and small-farmer-friendly food systems. In Mexico, Raramuri Indians marched into the governor's palace in 2008 to demand that genetically modified corn not contaminate their native seeds. La Via Campesina is part of a larger food sovereignty alliance because it turns out that we have concerned folks in the United States too.

So while there may be more awareness outside the United States that our life depends on seeds and that protecting them is in everyone's best interest, seed saving and mobilization for political change are active in the United States as well. Seed Savers Exchange is a nonprofit organization started in 1975 in which members pass on their garden heritage by collecting and distributing thousands of samples of rare garden seeds to other gardeners. Heritage Farm, an 890-acre farm in Iowa, is home to Seed Savers; thousands of heritage seeds are maintained and sold there. They function as a kind of US seed bank and are therefore part of our food security. Seed Savers' stated mission is "to conserve and promote America's culturally diverse but endangered garden and food crop heritage for future generations by collecting, growing, and sharing heirloom seeds and plants."[12]

In 2007, over five hundred people from eighty countries gathered for the Forum for Food Sovereignty in Selingue, Mali. Indigenous farmers, along with landless peoples, fisherfolk, rural workers, migrants, pastoralists, and environmental and urban movement representatives, joined together to define food sovereignty. One result was this declaration: "Food sovereignty is the right of peoples to healthy and culturally appropriate food produced through ecologically sound and sustainable methods, and their right to define their own food and agriculture systems. It puts the aspirations and needs of those who produce, distribute and consume food at the heart of food systems and policies rather than the demands of markets and corporations."[13]

The loudest words spoken from the global table are words of resistance. Most of the resistance seems to be about maintaining control over food—that is, fighting the loss of control associated with trading traditional seeds not owned by anyone (and free to everyone) for modified seeds owned and controlled by a few large and highly profitable corporations.

How to Be a Seed Keeper

Last spring our two-year-old granddaughter Eden spent the night during fava bean planting. I slipped her into the red T-shirt and tan Carhartt overalls that I keep on hand for farming and forest-exploring ventures. She grabbed the blue denim hat and plopped it on her head, and we headed out to the field. I hoed a trench and then squatted beside her and let her drop the large, smooth, flat, brown beans into the row. I squared them up and straightened them out, but she was the one planting the row—and she knew it. She was being a seed keeper.

Only some of us garden, but all of us eat; so any of us can be keepers of seeds, which means we are keepers of diversity. Here are three other ways—besides planting heirloom seeds yourself—to be seed keepers.

The first and easiest way we can protect diversity is to eat diversity, that is, to eat heirloom varieties, including pigs and chickens. Generally, heirloom varieties will cost more. Heirloom tomatoes don't travel or keep well, which is why tomatoes are genetically modified to help them tolerate transportation and last longer on the shelf. Heirloom breeds of pig are usually raised by farmers who treat them respectfully, feeding them their natural diet and housing them in a more natural habitat, which costs more than the alternative offered by CAFOs (concentrated animal feeding operations).

Does it seem ironic that something is *saved* by eating it? Eating Copia or Amarillo tomatoes, Gravenstein apples, and Duroc pigs ensures that farmers will keep growing and raising them. Species of plants (and animals) need to be cultivated to be saved. We have an interdependent relationship with seeds. They need us to nurture them; we need them to nurture us.

The second way to be a seed saver is related to the first: don't buy food products made from GM seed. Chiefly, this means corn and soy products, as well as canola oil, but this category also includes potatoes, zucchini, and tomatoes and will soon include wheat. While buying heirloom varieties ensures diversity, one can't buy heirloom corn flakes; but one can buy organic corn flakes. To be organic, by definition, means to be without genetic modification. When you buy organic soy milk, organic corn chips, and organic coffee or chocolate, you are supporting farmers who are committed to not using broad-spectrum pesticides, herbicides, and petroleum-based fertilizers and who are also planting non-GM seeds, keeping diversity alive and well.

A third way to be a seed saver is to become informed about efforts in your sphere of influence (local, state, and national) to get GM food labeled as such and to support farmers' efforts to maintain control of their seeds. Vermont, Maine, Connecticut, Rhode Island, Washington, California, Oregon, and Colorado have all passed, or are attempting to pass, legislation requiring GM foods be labeled. Monsanto is actively fighting back, and they have plenty of money at their disposal. They poured $9 million into Oregon and Colorado to defeat measures being voted on in November 2014. Monsanto already has an image problem, and to be required to label GM foods is like having to put the Surgeon General's warning on cigarettes—it suggests GM foods should be avoided by people who care about their health, food sovereignty, and the health of the planet.

Other efforts focus on keeping large seed companies accountable for negligence, primarily from the contamination of non-GM fields with Roundup Ready GM wheat seed. As of September 2014 it appeared that Monsanto was settling with Oregon and Kansas farmers for contaminating non-GM fields with GM wheat, a discovery made in 2013. Japan and South Korea are big importers of Oregon wheat. Once they heard about the GM-contaminated wheat, they canceled their contracts, at a significant financial loss to the farmers. How the seed got there is a mystery but is likely related to the wheat trials of GM seed that Monsanto ran in sixteen states, including Oregon, between 1998 and 2005. Theories range from sabotage and seed being carried by wind to harvested seed getting blended with other wheat seed that was put on the market for subsequent years. Whatever the cause, for the first time Monsanto is being held accountable for not taking precautions to ensure that their seed doesn't contaminate nearby fields. Other lawsuits are pending from farmers in Washington, Montana, and Idaho, who suspect Roundup Ready wheat has also contaminated their fields and who now have reason to believe Monsanto will be held responsible for negligence.

Since 1997 Monsanto has sued farmers who saved GM seed and replanted it. Farmers who buy from Monsanto enter a contractual agreement promising not to save the seed but to repurchase it every year. Monsanto has ways of checking compliance. They have been able to settle with about 700 noncompliant farmers out of court, but they have taken 145 to court. As of 2014 only nine cases had made it all the way through the system, and Monsanto reports that in every case the jury decided in Monsanto's favor.

That might change. The Oregon case is the first lawsuit against Monsanto for contamination. In 2013 Monsanto was required by federal courts to pay a $93 million settlement to residents of Nitro, West Virginia, for exposing them to the poison dioxin, which Monsanto produces there. Non-GMO activists are hopeful that these lawsuits will be the beginning of what holds Monsanto in check or brings them down as ordinary people begin to consider GM food a threat to our health, to our planet's health, and to food security.

A Final Word about Change

The world I was born into barely resembles the world I inhabit. Kids played at parks or in neighborhoods without parental supervision, doing "dangerous" things like climbing trees. Our phones were landlines connected to a wall, which were often party lines that we shared with one or two other families. Store registers went "Ka-ching! Ka-ching!" instead of "Beep! Beep!," and we had fewer cereal choices at the grocery store. Credit cards were uncommon, and there was no Starbucks and no Amazon .com—although we did have McDonald's and A&W. A sixty-minute television show had only nine minutes of commercials, and people didn't pick up and move nearly so often. In my world, kids grew up fearing a nuclear attack from Russia.

Change happens. Adaptation follows. Some of it is for the better and some for the worse; sometimes it's neither better nor worse. Plants and animals slowly adapt to changing environments. Social worlds change as countries and individuals gain and lose freedoms and adjust accordingly. Our ideas about the world change as we discover more about it—like the fact that we orbit the sun rather than the sun setting its course by us or the possibility that the way we live impacts the global climate. Beliefs change over time, influenced by a renewed understanding of what equality means in the twenty-first century, who we believe the marginalized are, and what the marginalized need for justice. How we define a family has changed over the millennia, as has our definition of the good life. Even faith and our expressions of faith change as we grow in understanding and worship together, as we learn to walk together as disciples.

Sociologists measure rates and degrees of change and agree that slow change in small increments over time is less disruptive to social (and physical) systems than rapid revolutionary change. Determining when to adapt and change and when to resist change and protect our heritage is perhaps a greater challenge in a time when change is so rapid; science makes so much possible in a very short time.

A few things will never change. God's love for us is immutable, and nothing can separate us from it. We can count on God's abiding presence in the world—that God is bringing to fullness what God began and that we are God's representatives on earth, stewards who are here to love mercy and do justice.

How does that relate to the small wonder of seeds? Is it overly sentimental to see seeds as offspring of the ages and to feel that I am holding something from the beginning of time when I cradle them in my hands? Certainly those seeds were different from the seeds I plant now, in the twenty-first century. They have adapted, over time, to changing climates and the changing habits of those who eat them. But they fed us then and feed us still. I am drawn toward protecting a process that has fed humanity since the beginning, even if it makes me a bit of a naysayer in terms of progress and raises other hard-to-answer questions.

As stewards, may we collectively keep seeds safe—the seeds of our faith, the seeds of our knowledge about how to live well, and the seeds of the foods that feed us. May we keep them safe for our children and our grandchildren's grandchildren, in honor of our parents and the foreparents who kept them safe for us. In the keeping, may we see the Seed Maker who began it all with a Word-seed spoken into the void—the God who holds the fullness of all it will become.

• *Hazelnut Honey Wheat Bread* •

2 tbsp.	yeast
½ c. plus 1¾ c.	water
1 scant tbsp.	salt

½ c.   honey

¼ c.   oil or softened butter

6–7 c.   whole wheat flour

2 tbsp. gluten (optional)

⅓ c.   flax seeds

½ c.   each of sunflower
         seeds and chopped roasted
         hazelnuts

In a large bowl proof yeast in ½ cup warm water (that is, let the yeast "sit" with the water for 5–10 minutes to soften). In a separate bowl combine 1¾ cup warm water, salt, honey, and oil or butter.

Once the yeast is bubbly, add the liquids, 2 cups whole wheat flour, and the optional gluten (it helps 100% whole wheat bread rise better). Mix or blend with a wooden spoon or mixer.

Add another 4–5 cups flour, ½ cup flour at a time until the dough (which will be sticky) holds together. Add flax seeds, sunflower seeds, and hazelnuts.

Turn out on a well-floured surface and knead in more flour as needed until you have a stiff dough. Knead another 8–10 minutes. Place dough in a greased bowl and cover with a hot damp dishcloth and then cover that with a tea towel. Let rise until doubled in size (about 1½ hours).

Punch down the dough, divide it in half, cover, and let it rest 10 minutes. Meanwhile, grease 2 loaf pans and sprinkle corn meal or oats on the bottom of each pan. Hand pat each half into a rectangle about 1 inch thick and then roll it up into a log. Pinch the bottom seam shut, fold the ends under, and place each loaf in a pan. Cover with a tea towel and let rise until doubled in size (about 45 minutes).

During the last part of this second rise, preheat the oven to 375 degrees. Bake for about 45 minutes, covering with foil for the last 20 minutes if the tops brown too much. Cool slightly in the pan before removing to cool completely on racks. Best served warm with real butter.

Reflections and Questions

1. The chapter comes close to apologizing for wondering whether it is sentimental to view seeds as the offspring of the ages. But Jesus was the seed of David, and some of Jesus's most powerful parables are

centered on seeds. Maybe we have become unused to connecting very real-life with spiritual metaphor. How do you experience this real-life connection of seeds to who you are today—to the life you have and to your faith, values, and habits? How does it raise your level of respect for what came before to consider how you are an offspring of the ages?

2. Related to the previous question, does this chapter change the way you see seeds as the full, visual, embodiment of all that gets carried from one generation to the next? If so, does that make seeds themselves and protecting them seem more important?

3. What made Jesus's seed parables powerful in his day? (See the parable of the sower, the story of the wheat and the weeds, and the illustration of the mustard seed in Matthew 13 and Mark 4.) Do you think these parables are more powerful to farmers and vegetable and flower gardeners than to people who don't grow food? Has reading this chapter deepened the richness of these parables?

4. People often seek perspective from those whom they expect will agree with them. This chapter talks about going to the global table to enrich one's perspective on GM seeds. More broadly, it talks about the usefulness of seeking perspective in one's community rather than trying to determine a thing by oneself and of being willing to go outside typical sources for wisdom and perspective. Where do you go when you need perspective, and why do you go there? Why do you think it is generally difficult for people to choose to go outside normal networks and sources for information?

5. Speaking of other perspectives, how compelled are you by the GM seed story? What information was new to you? What questions does it raise for you, and how might you get them answered?

6. If you *are* compelled, what would it take to begin to be a seed saver of some sort? Buying heirloom tomatoes or apples? Supporting a rancher raising Duroc pigs? Planting an heirloom variety of squash in your vegetable garden?

7. This chapter talks about change and lists things that have changed in recent decades—some good, some bad, and some neutral. What are some of the good changes you've seen in your lifetime, including inventions, ideas, and possibly a return to traditions? Can you see

how the cycle of change and adaptation reflects those things of God that never change, like God's love and abiding presence? How does seeing God's consistency help comfort fears associated with change?

8. What is something ordinary that you relish or maybe just depend on? Can you find God in it and then find it worth a kind of attention that reclaims this ordinary thing as a daily grace?

Epilogue

Back to the Kitchen

"When you wake up in the morning, Pooh," said Piglet at last, "what's the first thing you say to yourself?"

"What's for breakfast?" said Pooh. "What do you say, Piglet?"

"I say, I wonder what's going to happen exciting today?" said Piglet.

Pooh nodded thoughtfully. "It's the same thing," he said.

—A. A. Milne, *Winnie the Pooh*

We've been observing the autumn equinox with a gathering of friends for almost a decade now. I'm sitting up in the tree house (again) with the remnants of our most recent celebration scattered around me. A string of lights is draped over the branches that hold up the tree house. I've taken down the candlelit lanterns, and the tables and chairs that we used up in the tree house are stacked by the ladder, ready to go down.

Truth is, I'm not quite ready to let go of the magic of Friday evening. It's not just that I can still taste the sautéed heirloom cherry tomatoes and basil or the butternut squash ravioli with sage browned butter and the pumpkin bread pudding with dulce de leche, though certainly that sustaining, delicious food was part of our exquisite evening.

Another part of the magic was preparing the food, which had begun two days prior with the pumpkin bread pudding and dulce de leche sauce. We needed the head start since Thursday is a harvest day, making it more about getting food in from the fields and into the hands of our community

199

supported agriculture (CSA) members than about getting it onto anyone's dinner plate.

Our apprentice Kara assisted in creating our autumn equinox celebration. The ideas to use little jars of honey with our guests' names on them as place markers (and parting gifts) and to sink carrots into a jar of water before adding flowers were hers.

So was eating in the tree house, though we both knew it would require descending and ascending the ladder to serve the main course after the salads, then again for dessert, and then again for hot tea, not to mention the tables, chairs, plates, glasses, linens, and lanterns.

Another layer of what made the evening wonderful was hearing conversation unfold between nine people, most of whom were connected through Mark and me. Several have now become Facebook friends with each other; I'd like to think they will become friends that might see each other again, maybe even host each other in their own homes.

At one point during dinner, Mark asked me to explain what the Slow Food Movement is, and mostly I said, "It's what we're doing right now." We were eating local and seasonal food that took a good while to prepare by two people who loved preparing it. We ate slowly and with intention; we savored our food. At one point Liz, who had had a rather complicated and hard week, interrupted the table conversation to say, "This is feeding my soul in a very significant way. Every single bite." As eating should.

And so we come full circle, back to the kitchen. Back to the shared table.

Evenings like this reinforce the vision that Mark and I share to bring people together, to grow affection for place, community, and food. The journey has spiritually formed not only Mark and me in powerful ways but also others—most profoundly our apprentices and interns, who have spent time at Fern Creek alongside us.

You don't have to run a farm or throw parties in tree houses for this to happen. To be spiritually formed is to put ourselves in places where God can order our passions, aligning them so that we care about the things God cares about. To be spiritually formed is to journey toward Jesus, toward being more *like* Jesus, living lives that grow to reflect God's image within us. We seek to be like Jesus for our own sake, but equally for the sake of others.

In the Sermon on the Mount, Jesus calls his followers to something more than pithy quotes and simple answers to complex questions. He calls for nuance and an examination of rationalizations and justifications. I borrow (and revised) the following from a talk Mark gave to college students this fall, in which he imagined something Jesus might say to us today.

"You have heard it said, 'Eat dark chocolate for it gladdens the heart and is good for you.' But I say, those whose hearts are gladdened through the oppression of the poor have forsaken justice."

Strong words, although not a direct quote. Still, Jesus spoke similarly strong words, and in doing so he made people uncomfortable. Along the way he also made enemies, but he loved them.

Eating is soul forming, but it seldom shows up in a list of spiritual disciplines that encourage us to grow in grace and to open ourselves up to the heart of God. A spiritual discipline of eating seems as profound as practicing worship, fasting, simplicity, study, compassion, service, or celebration. Might it not wrap its way around and through many if not all of these endeavors?

Every time we eat we make choices that impact some part of creation, including ourselves. With the grace and power of God we can choose simple, soul-forming choices (which are sometimes costly), like buying only fair-trade chocolate or meat that comes from animals raised in compassionate ways. Or we might choose to eat less meat and more vegetables, fruit, nuts, and grains grown closer to home. Putting up a jar or two of dilly beans in the summer or raspberry jam or salsa can be soul forming, helping us to be mindful of summer's bounty come winter, of the sustaining power of preserved food when the earth has less to offer. Making room for people in our kitchens and around our tables forms our souls. Might even supporting local farmers and beekeepers and seed keepers of all kinds lead to soul-forming growth?

Soul-forming food choices will likely lead us toward greater gratitude, generosity, hospitality, and maybe even truth-telling about little-known agricultural practices.

But remember: soul forming is not so much about you or me becoming more spiritually mature or somehow better people and more pleasing to God. Soul forming is about God. It is about recognizing and living out of God's deep, deep love. In the recognition of such amazing love, how could we not love what God loves and want what God wants? How could we not long to see a world flourishing, becoming the fullness God envisioned?

Dear God, make it so. Teach us to love what you love.

Reflections and Questions

1. If being spiritually formed is to put ourselves in places where God can order our passions, where we journey toward Jesus for our own sake and for the sake of others, how can food become part of that? Reflect on how food choices you make daily impact your inner life, your outward expressions of faith, and your relationship with God.

2. Final reflection: What two or three ideas have had the most impact on you? If you have found yourself compelled by anything, write down three things that you will begin to do differently, making one of them something that you will begin this week. What will help you sustain your choice? Perhaps doing it with a friend or bringing family members into the conversation? Perhaps it would help to reflect on and write down where you want to be or what you want to know and be doing in three months, six months, and/or a year.

Recommended Reading

Food Preparation and Cookbooks

Adler, Tamar. *An Everlasting Meal: Cooking with Economy and Grace*. New York: Scribner, 2012.

Campbell, LeAnn, and Stephen Campbell Disla. *The China Study Cookbook*. Dallas: BenBella Books, 2013.

FairShare CSA Coalition. *From Asparagus to Zucchini: A Guide to Cooking Farm-Fresh Seasonal Produce*. 3rd ed. Madison, WI: MACSAC, 2004.

Lappé, Frances. *A Diet for a Small Planet*. New York: Ballantine, 1971.

Lind, Mary Beth, and Cathleen Hockman-Wert. *Simply in Season: A World Community Cookbook*. Scottdale, PA: Herald Press, 2005.

Longacre, Doris. *More-with-Less: A World Community Cookbook*. Scottdale, PA: Herald Press, 1976.

Robertson, Robin. *Vegan Planet*. Cambridge, MA: Harvard Common Press, 2003.

Segersten, Alissa, and Tom Malterre. *Nourishing Meals: Healthy Gluten-Free Recipes for the Whole Family*. Bellingham, WA: Whole Life Press, 2012.

Witty, Helen, and Elizabeth Schneider Colchie. *Better Than Store-Bought: A Cookbook—Authoritative Recipes for the Foods That Most People Never Knew They Could Make at Home*. New York: Harper & Row, 1979.

Food Preservation

Bubel, Nancy, and Mike Bubel. *Root Cellaring: Natural Cold Storage of Fruits and Vegetables*. 2nd ed. Pownal, VT: Storey, 1991.

Krisoff, Liana. *Canning for a New Generation: Bold, Fresh Flavors for the Modern Pantry*. New York: Stewart, Tabori & Chang, 2010.

McClellan, Marisa. *Food in Jars: Preserving in Small Batches Year-Round*. Philadelphia: Running Press, 2012.

Rombauer, Irma S., and Marion Rombauer Becker. *The Joy of Cooking*. 75th anniversary ed. New York: Scribner, 2006. This book first came out in 1931 and is still being revised.

Vinton, Sheri Brooks. *Put 'em Up!* North Adams, MA: Storey, 2010.

Food and Health

Buettner, Dan. *The Blue Zones Solution: Eating and Living Like the World's Healthiest People*. Washington, DC: National Geographic, 2015.

Campbell, T. Colin, and Thomas M. Campbell II. *The China Study: The Most Comprehensive Study of Nutrition Ever Conducted and the Startling Implications for Diet, Weight Loss, and Long-Term Health*. Dallas: BenBella Books, 2006.

Davis, William. *Wheat Belly: Lose the Wheat, Lose the Weight and Find Your Path Back to Health*. New York: Rodale Books, 2014.

Pollan, Michael. *In Defense of Food: An Eater's Manifesto*. New York: Penguin, 2008.

Schlosser, Eric. *Fast Food Nation: The Dark Side of the All-American Meal*. New York: Perennial, 2001.

Smith, Jeffrey M. *Seeds of Deception: Exposing Industry and Government Lies about the Safety of the Genetically Engineered Foods You're Eating*. Fairfield, IA: Yes! Books, 2003.

Food and Farming

Berry, Wendell. *Hannah Coulter*. Berkeley: Counterpoint, 2004.

———. *Sex, Economy, Freedom & Community: Eight Essays*. New York: Pantheon, 1993.

Eisnitz, Gail. *Slaughterhouse: The Shocking Story of Greed, Neglect, and Inhumane Treatment inside the U.S. Meat Industry*. Amherst, NY: Prometheus, 1997.

Kingsolver, Barbara. *Small Wonders*. New York: Perennial, 2002.

Ray, Janisse. *The Seed Underground: A Growing Revolution to Save Food*. White River Junction, VT: Chelsea Green, 2012.

Food and Faith

Bahnson, Fred. *Soil and Sacrament: A Spiritual Memoir of Food and Faith*. New York: Simon & Schuster, 2013.

Fields, Leslie Leyland, ed. *The Spirit of Food*. Eugene, OR: Wipf and Stock, 2010.

Stone, Rachel Marie. *Eat with Joy: Redeeming God's Gift of Food*. Downers Grove, IL: InterVarsity, 2013.

Wirzba, Norman. *Food & Faith: A Theology of Eating*. Cambridge: Cambridge University Press, 2011.

Food and Culture

Brett, Brian. *Trauma Farm: A Rebel History of Rural Life*. Vancouver: Greystone, 2009.

Kimball, Kristen. *The Dirty Life: On Farming, Food, and Love*. New York: Scribner, 2010.

Marks, Susan. *Finding Betty Crocker: The Secret Life of America's First Lady of Food*. Minneapolis: University of Minnesota Press, 2007.

Pollan, Michael. *Cooked: A Natural History of Transformation*. New York: Penguin, 2013.

———. *The Omnivore's Dilemma: A Natural History of Four Meals*. New York: Penguin, 2006.

Notes

Introduction

1. Leslie Leyland Fields, *The Spirit of Food* (Eugene, OR: Wipf and Stock, 2010), xxiii.

Chapter 1 The Common Table

1. Norman Wirzba, *Food and Faith: A Theology of Eating* (New York: Cambridge University Press, 2011), 11.

2. James Fallows, "The 50 Greatest Breakthroughs since the Wheel," *The Atlantic*, November 2013, 56–68.

3. In the mid-twentieth century the introduction of synthetic fertilizer, pesticides, and (later) high-yielding crops resulted in the ability of farmers everywhere to significantly increase crop production. This "green revolution" was a hopeful solution to end world hunger but is increasingly criticized as unsustainable, bad for people, and bad for ecosystems. The inventions of the green revolution are being rejected by people around the world and quite fervently by those from countries in the Global South.

4. Alistair Moffat quoted in Hannah Furness, "How a Bowl of Porridge Transformed Mankind," *The Telegraph*, June 28, 2013, http://www.telegraph.co.uk/science/science-news/10148594/How-a-bowl-of-porridge-transformed-mankind.html.

5. Michael Pollan, *Cooked: A Natural History of Transformation* (New York: Penguin, 2013), 111.

6. Chris Colin and Carol Pott, *The Blue Pages: A Directory of Companies Rated by Their Politics and Practices* (Sausalito, CA: PoliPoint Press, 2006), 69.

7. "How Americans Eat Today," *CBS News* video, 4:40, January 12, 2010, http://www.cbsnews.com/news/how-americans-eat-today/.

8. Jason K. Mitchell, "Marital Dining Practices: Affecting Change in Marital Satisfaction through Marital Self-Efficacy" (PsyD diss., George Fox University, 2012).

9. Wirzba, *Food and Faith*, 11.

10. Rachel Marie Stone, *Eat with Joy: Redeeming God's Gift of Food* (Downers Grove, IL: InterVarsity, 2013), 76. Italics in original.

11. I recommend chap. 5 in Wirzba's book, *Food and Faith*, for an excellent discussion of these ways and purposes.

12. Wirzba, *Food and Faith*, 145. Italics in original.

Chapter 2 Cooking: Artful Transformations

1. For a good history of feeding soldiers, see "Army Operational Rations: Historical Background," US Army Quartermaster Foundation, accessed June 21, 2015, www.qmfound.com/army_rations_historical_background.htm.

2. US Department of Labor, Bureau of Labor Statistics, "Employment Characteristics of Families Summary," news release, April 23, 2015, www.bls.gov/news.release/famee.nr0.htm.

3. Kevin Murray, "Bosch Survey: What's Keeping You Out of the Kitchen?," *Purcell Murray Blog*, October 26, 2011, www.purcellmurray.com/blog/index.php/article/5201.

4. Harris Polls, "Three in Ten Americans Love to Cook, While One in Five Do Not Enjoy It or Don't Cook," July 27, 2010, Harris Interactive, www.harrisinteractive.com/NewsRoom/HarrisPolls/tabid/447/mid/1508/articleId/444/ctl/ReadCustom%20Default/Default.aspx.

5. Cooking Matters/No Kid Hungry, "It's Dinnertime: A Report on Low-Income Families' Efforts to Plan, Shop for and Cook Healthy Meals," CookingMatters.org, 2011, www.nokidhungry.org/images/cm-study/report-highlights.pdf.

6. Norman Wirzba, *Food and Faith: A Theology of Eating* (New York: Cambridge University Press, 2011), xiii.

7. Wendell Berry, "Conservation Is Good Work," in *Sex, Economy, Freedom & Community* (New York: Pantheon Books, 1993), 35.

8. I appreciated the thoughtfulness of Brandon and Michael, and their willingness to spend an hour conversing over tea at Chapters (Newberg, Oregon) in February 2014.

9. Mary Oliver, "Messenger," in *Thirst* (Boston: Beacon, 2006), 1.

Chapter 3 Preservation

1. Henri J. M. Nouwen, *Show Me the Way: Readings for Each Day of Lent* (New York: Crossroads, 1992), 13.

2. Preservation Shares are an add-on we offer to five CSA members. These members get extra fruit and vegetables for preserving, plus dried beans, honey, and a class in preservation techniques. Our hope is to inspire and help others to eat more locally year-round, aided by food they've put up themselves in the summer and fall.

3. A great resource for anyone with a desire to store some seasonal vegetables is Nancy and Mike Bubel's book, *Root Cellaring: Natural Cold Storage of Fruits and Vegetables* (North Adams, MA: Storey, 1991).

4. Wendell Berry, "It All Turns on Affection," 41st Annual Jefferson Lecture on the Humanities, John F. Kennedy Center for the Performing Arts, April 2012, transcript and video recording, TV Worldwide, 77:30, www.onbeing.org/blog/wendell-berry-says-it-all-turns-affection/4638.

5. Frederick Buechner, *The Sacred Journey: A Memoir of Early Days* (San Francisco: Harper SanFrancisco, 1982), 112.

6. Eugene H. Peterson, *A Long Obedience in the Same Direction: Discipleship in an Instant Society* (Downers Grove, IL: InterVarsity, 1980).

7. Copied from Nathan's handwritten letter (October 2014).

8. Nouwen, *Show Me the Way*, 15.

9. Chun Z. Yang, Stuart I. Yaniger, V. Craig Jordan, Daniel J. Klein, and George D. Bittner, "Most Plastic Products Release Estrogenic Chemicals: A Potential Health Problem That Can Be Solved," *Environmental Health Perspectives* 119 (July 2011): 989–96.

Chapter 4 Eating Closer to Home: On Being Neighborly

1. Printed on a brochure at Our Lady of Guadalupe Trappist Abbey in Carlton, Oregon.

2. Russell Schweickart, "No Frames, No Boundaries: Connecting with the Whole Planet—from Space," in *Rediscovering The North American Vision, In Context* 3 (Summer 1983): 16, http:www.context.org/iclib/ic03/schweick/. You can also watch Schweickart talk about his

experience online: "Astronaut Rusty Schweickart Opens Up to the Experience," YouTube video, 2:41, posted on July 15, 2010, www.youtube.com/watch?v=6Zlr5G2kp6g.

3. For more information visit www.cultivatekc.org.

4. Steven McFaddan, "Vandana Shiva: Cultivating Diversity, Freedom and Hope," Cornucopia Institute, April 25, 2014, Cornucopia.org/2014/04/vandana-shiva-cultivating-diversity -freedom-hope/. McFaddan's article is a report on Shiva's presentation to The Call of the Land Conference in Kansas.

5. Norman Wirzba, *Food and Faith: A Theology of Eating* (New York: Cambridge University Press, 2011), 72. Italics in original.

6. According to the scientific community, climate change is undeniable and brought about by human causes. While not everyone finds the science compelling, the geologists, climatologists, and other earth scientists do. I'm inclined to trust them over businesses with interests to protect.

7. The Global South refers to countries in Africa, Latin America, developing Asia, and the Middle East, making up 133 out of the 197 countries of the world.

8. Go to www.earth-policy.org to access Earth Policy Institute's homepage and links to full-text books and articles.

9. See Megan Bedard, "5 Astonishing Facts about the Food We Throw in the Trash," takepart (website), January 11, 2013, www.takepart.com/photos/food-waste-facts/food-waste-facts, for a good exploration of related issues concerning food waste.

10. Rachel Marie Stone, *Eat with Joy* (Downers Grove, IL: InterVarsity, 2013), 166–67.

11. Malinda Geisler, "Commodity Apple Profile," Agricultural Marketing Resource Center, last updated December 2013, http://www.agmrc.org/commodities_products/fruits/apples /commodity-apple-profile/.

12. This is based on a 2001 study with data collected from 1981 to 1998. In that time period the numbers of miles increased, so those quantities might have changed since then. Rich Pirog, Timothy Van Pelt, Kamyar Enshayan, and Ellen Cook, "Food, Fuel, and Freeways: An Iowa Perspective on How Far Food Travels, Fuel Usage, and Greenhouse Gas Emissions," Leopold Center for Sustainable Agriculture, Iowa State University, June 2001, leopold.iastate.edu/sites /default/files/pubs-and-papers/2011-06-food-fuel-and-freeways-iowa-perspective-how-far-food -travels-fuel-usage-and-greenhouse-gas-emissions.pdf.

13. One cow raised in the West releases 120 kg of methane gas per year (which compares to 60 kg for cows raised elsewhere in the world), 1.5 kg for a pig, 0.12 kg for a person, .015 kg for a chicken, and zero for a tomato plant. In fact, the tomato plant reabsorbs some of that CO_2. See "How Does Agriculture Contribute to Climate Change?," World Future Council, worldfuturecouncil.org/2326.html.

14. Wikipedia is a great place to gather information about an assortment of farming practices. In general, the information is stated more neutrally than what one would find from the Humane Society, PETA, or other animal welfare groups. Not that I'm supporting neutrality here, but Wikipedia offers a bigger picture, with information contributed and edited by multiple sources.

15. Watch this video on *Slate* for an interesting look at how much Walmart would need to raise its prices so that it could pay workers enough *not* to qualify for SNAP benefits: "If Wal-Mart Paid Its Employees a Living Wage, How Much Would Prices Go Up?," *Slate* video, 2:02, April 1, 2014, www.slate.com/articles/business/moneybox/2014/04/big_box_stores_make_billions _off_food_stamps_often_it_s_their_own_workers.html.

16. Rick Unger, "Wal-Mart Returning to Full-Time Workers—Obamacare Not Such a Job Killer After All?," *Forbes*, September 25, 2013, www.forbes.com/sites/rickungar/2013/09/25 /wal-mart-returning-to-full-time-workers-obamacare-not-such-a-job-killer-after-all/.

17. Anthony Zurcher, "Wal-Mart's Insurance Move Reveals Obamacare Truth," BBC, October 8, 2014, www.bbc.com/news/blogs-echochambers-29544149.

18. Stephanie Clifford, "Wal-Mart Is Fined $82 Million over Mishandling of Hazardous Wastes," *New York Times*, May 28, 2013, www.nytimes.com/2013/05/29/business/wal-mart-is
-fined-82-million-over-mishandling-of-hazardous-wastes.html?_r=0.

19. Ibid.

20. "Whole Foods Co-CEO: Executive Pay Caps a Part of Our 'Culture,'" *Huffington Post*, June 18, 2013, huffingtonpost.com/2013/06/18/walter-robb-salary_n_3459029.html.

21. Bonnie Kavoussi, "Walmart's CEO Paid 1,034 Times More Than the Median Walmart Worker: PayScale," *Huffington Post*, March 29, 2013, huffingtonpost.com/2013/03/29/walmart
-ceo-pay_n_2978180.html.

22. McFaddan, "Vandana Shiva."

23. Interview with Brenda Berg, March 2015.

24. Check out Sarah's blog at www.mydarlingvegan.com.

25. Frances Moore Lappé, "The Food Movement: Its Power and Possibilities," *The Nation*, September 14, 2011, www.thenation.com/article/163403/food-movement-its-power-and-possibilities.

Chapter 5 Harvesting: Labors of Love

1. Mary Oliver, *Swan: Poems and Prose Poems* (Boston: Beacon, 2012).

2. Elizabeth Nauman, Mark VanLandingham, Philip Anglewicz, Umaporn Patthavanit, and Sureeporn Punpuing, "Rural-to-Urban Migration and Changes in Health among Young Adults in Thailand," *Demography* 52 (February 2015), www.uclouvain.be/cps/ucl/doc/demo
/documents/Nauman_VanLandingham_Anglewicz_Patthavanit_Punpuing.pdf.

3. The latest Global Climate and Catastrophe Report can be accessed at http://thoughtleader
ship.aonbenfield.com/sitepages/display.aspx?tl=460.

4. Norman Wirzba, *Food and Faith: A Theology of Eating* (New York: Cambridge University Press, 2011), 110–11.

5. Gail Eisnitz, *Slaughterhouse: The Shocking Story of Greed, Neglect, and Inhumane Treatment inside the U.S. Meat Industry* (Amherst, NY: Prometheus Books, 1997), 87.

6. Jennifer Dillard, "Slaughterhouse Nightmare: Psychological Harm Suffered by Slaughterhouse Employees and the Possibility of Redress through Legal Reform," *Georgetown Journal on Poverty Law & Policy* 15, no. 2 (Summer 2008): 391–408.

7. See Food Empowerment Project for a more thorough description of the group and what it is attempting to accomplish: www.foodispower.org.

8. Sue Monk Kidd, *The Invention of Wings* (New York: Viking, 2014), 184.

9. Julian of Norwich, *Revelations of Divine Love*, trans. Elizabeth Spearing (London: Penguin, 1999), 58.

10. Ibid.

11. Ibid.

12. To learn more about Food Alliance, which works to support sustainability in food and agriculture, check out their webpage at www.foodalliance.org.

13. Wendell Berry, *Sex, Economy, Freedom & Community* (New York: Pantheon, 1992), 24.

Chapter 6 In the Garden

1. Norman Wirzba, *Food and Faith: A Theology of Eating* (New York: Cambridge University Press, 2011), 100.

2. Ibid., 138.

3. Richard Foster, Lynne M. Baab, and Ruth Haley Barton, to name a few.

4. Forward Movement is a ministry of the Episcopal Church whose mission is to reinvigorate the life of the church. Much of this is done through devotionals and books that promote spiritual growth.

5. This prayer by Phillip Brooks (1835–93) is used quarterly in *Forward Day By Day* (Cincinnati: Forward Movement).

6. Eliot Wigginton, ed., *Foxfire 4: Fiddle Making, Springhouses, Horse Trading, Sassafras Tea, Berry Buckets, Gardening* (Garden City, NY: Anchor, 1977), 204, 207.

7. While this is a line from Mary Oliver's poem "Sometimes," this theme and words like them run throughout her poetry and essays. "Sometimes" is from *Red Bird* (Boston: Beacon, 2008), 36.

Chapter 7 Seeds: Fullness in the Hands of God

1. Janisse Ray, *The Seed Underground: A Growing Revolution to Save Food* (White River Junction, VT: Chelsea Green, 2012), xiv.

2. *Food sovereignty* was first used as a term in 1996 by members of Via Campesina. It began as a movement of indigenous people striving for the right to define their own food systems and has grown into a global campaign.

3. See omri.org for further information.

4. Department of Soil and Crop Sciences, "Transgenetic Crops: An Introduction and Resource Guide," University of Colorado, last updated January 29, 2004, http://cls.casa.colostate.edu/transgeniccrops/history.html.

5. United States Department of Agriculture, "Report on Adoption of Genetically Engineered Crops in the U.S.," last updated July 14, 2014, http://www.ers.usda.gov/data-products/adoption-of-genetically-engineered-crops-in-the-us.aspx#.VBh7xFb6K9Y.

6. Damian Carrington, "GM Crops Good for Environment, Study Finds," *The Guardian*, June 13, 2012, http://www.theguardian.com/environment/2012/jun/13/gm-crops-environment-study.

7. Barbara Kingsolver, "Fist in the Eye of God," in *Small Wonders* (New York: Perennial, 2002), 100–101.

8. H. C. Van den Broeck et al., "Presence of Celiac Disease Epitopes in Modern and Old Hexaploid Wheat Varieties: Wheat Breeding May Have Contributed to Increased Prevalence of Celiac Disease," *Theoretical and Applied Genetics* 121, no. 8 (November 2010), http://www.ncbi.nlm.nih.gov/pmc/articles/PMC2963738/.

9. Amy Dean and Jennifer Armstrong, "Statement on Genetically Modified Foods," American Academy of Environmental Medicine, May 8, 2009, https://www.aaemonline.org/gmo.php.

10. For a good summary of Vandana Shiva's environmental efforts and the controversy in India, check out Michael Specter's article "Seeds of Doubt," *New Yorker*, August 25, 2014, www.newyorker.com/magazine/2014/08/25/seeds-of-doubt.

11. Go to www.navdanya.org for a fuller sense of the network's goals and activities—and to be inspired.

12. See seedsavers.org to learn more about Seed Savers Exchange programs and seeds.

13. For more information, see "Declaration of Nyéléni," *Nyéléni*, March 27, 2007, nyeleni.org/spip.php?article290.